T0259712

SpringerBriefs on Cyber Security Systems and Networks

Editor-in-chief

Yang Xiang, Digital Research & Innovation Capability Platform, Swinburne University of Technology, Hawthorn, Melbourne, VIC, Australia

Series editors

Liqun Chen, University of Surrey, Guildford, UK
Kim-Kwang Raymond Choo, Department of Information Systems and Cyber Security, University of Texas at San Antonio, San Antonio, TX, USA
Sherman S. M. Chow, Department of Information Engineering, The Chinese University of Hong Kong, Hong Kong
Robert H. Deng, School of Information Systems, Singapore Management University, Singapore, Singapore
Dieter Gollmann, Hamburg University of Technology, Hamburg, Germany
Javier Lopez, University of Malaga, Malaga, Spain
Kui Ren, University at Buffalo, Buffalo, NY, USA
Jianying Zhou, Singapore University of Technology and Design, Singapore, Singapore

The series aims to develop and disseminate an understanding of innovations, paradigms, techniques, and technologies in the contexts of cyber security systems and networks related research and studies. It publishes thorough and cohesive overviews of state-of-the-art topics in cyber security, as well as sophisticated techniques, original research presentations and in-depth case studies in cyber systems and networks. The series also provides a single point of coverage of advanced and timely emerging topics as well as a forum for core concepts that may not have reached a level of maturity to warrant a comprehensive textbook. It addresses security, privacy, availability, and dependability issues for cyber systems and networks, and welcomes emerging technologies, such as artificial intelligence, cloud computing, cyber physical systems, and big data analytics related to cyber security research. The mainly focuses on the following research topics:

Fundamentals and Theories

- Cryptography for cyber security
- Theories of cyber security
- Provable security

Cyber Systems and Networks

- Cyber systems Security
- Network security
- Security services
- Social networks security and privacy
- Cyber attacks and defense
- Data-driven cyber security
- Trusted computing and systems

Applications and Others

- Hardware and device security
- Cyber application security
- Human and social aspects of cyber security

More information about this series at http://www.springer.com/series/15797

Darren Quick · Kim-Kwang Raymond Choo

Big Digital Forensic Data

Volume 1: Data Reduction Framework and Selective Imaging

 Springer

Darren Quick
University of South Australia
Adelaide, SA
Australia

Kim-Kwang Raymond Choo
University of Texas at San Antonio
San Antonio, TX
USA

ISSN 2522-5561   ISSN 2522-557X (electronic)
SpringerBriefs on Cyber Security Systems and Networks
ISBN 978-981-10-7762-3   ISBN 978-981-10-7763-0   (eBook)
https://doi.org/10.1007/978-981-10-7763-0

Library of Congress Control Number: 2018934398

Printed on acid-free paper

This Springer imprint is published by the registered company Springer Nature Singapore Pte Ltd.
part of Springer Nature
The registered company address is: 152 Beach Road, #21-01/04 Gateway East, Singapore 189721,
Singapore

Foreword

"Work smarter not harder." So goes the age old adage. Unfortunately, we in the digital forensics community have continued to work harder and harder over the years—developing distributed computing models and tools, leveraging collaboration platforms, and mastering the task force approach to large scale investigation and analysis. This isn't to say the community hasn't benefited from increasingly "smart" tools and people. Our community is full of superb tool developers and a highly skilled, technically adept community of investigators. "Smart" surely isn't a quality lacking in our field, as I continue to be impressed with technically adept practitioners, researchers, and tool developers.

The future also looks bright as I peer years ahead, anticipating an increasingly smart suite of tools that more fully leverage the machine learning wave that's gaining momentum and finding its rightful place in our field. I look forward to the day, in the not too distant future, where the analyst's toolkit transcends the simple 'search, extract, and present' paradigm of old and begins to truly reduce the analytical burden and overhead that still plagues today's investigators. Yet today, we seem to be stuck at the dangerous intersection of "collect and search every literal bit of evidence" and "storage capacity and use eclipses modern, common place processing capabilities." And in my view, simply throwing additional compute at the problem, to index and present voluminous amounts of data to the investigator faster isn't the right solution. We are drowning in a deluge of data, more and more every day.

This book not only provides a great review and critical analysis of the current literature surrounding big data forensics, it provides useful and paradigm shifting frameworks for approaching the problem we face today—where the amount of data far eclipses the intelligence of our analytical platforms. Simply put, in this book, Drs. Quick and Choo provide transformative frameworks for selective imaging, quick analysis, and intelligence driven information fusion. This book provides mechanisms, backed up by empirical studies, to work smarter not harder in answering investigative questions today. Thankfully, they do so while remaining mindful of the need to preserve evidence for more in-depth analysis.

In this book, the authors provide useful frameworks that *augment* current approaches, not replace them. They provide frameworks that make investigations more effective and efficient. They provide a compelling argument for changing the way we currently do business. In short, anyone interested in advancing the field of big data forensics will find this book a great resource for surveying the field. I hope and expect this book will facilitate greater discussion of the big data challenges and solutions thereto in the very important field of digital investigations.

San Antonio, USA   Nicole Beebe, Ph.D., CISSP, CCFP, EnCE, ACE
                                                  Director, The Cyber Center for Security and
                                          Analytics, Associate Professor of Cyber Security,
                                          The University of Texas at San Antonio (Computer
                                              Crime Investigator, U.S. Air Force Office of Special
                                                             Investigations 1998–2007)

Preface

Digital forensic analysis is the process of identification, preservation, analysis, and presentation of digital and electronic evidence in a manner that is legally acceptable. A major challenge to digital forensic analysis is the ongoing growth in the volume of data seized and presented for analysis. This is a result of the continuing development of storage technology, consumer devices, and cloud storage, which has led to increasing backlogs of evidence awaiting analysis, often many months to years, affecting even the largest digital forensic labs.

There have been many calls for research to address the volume challenge. While more people are needed to undertake analysis, there is also a potential to develop innovative methods to collect relevant data to conduct analysis, reducing the time a practitioner spends sorting the wheat from the chaff, or looking for needles in ever-growing haystacks. Data mining is a process of knowledge discovery which may offer a faster way to understand the ever-increasing volume of data. Applying the process of data mining to digital forensic data may lead to a methodology to assist practitioners in analyzing the vast volumes of data.

The research outlined herein involved collecting and assembling a corpus of test data from a range of devices: mobile phones, portable storage, and computers, as well as other sources of digital forensic data. Research was then undertaken using the collected data in relation to applying data reduction and intelligence analysis methodologies to determine which, if any, are applicable to digital forensic analysis.

In the following book, a framework for data mining and data reduction is outlined, including a methodology for data reduction, which paves the way for Volume 2, in which a process of quick analysis, in-depth analysis, semi-automated information and entity extraction, and link charting in conjunction with link analysis is outlined. In Volume 1, the framework is explained, and then applied to a test data corpus and real-world data to ensure the process is valid and applicable to real-world data and investigations.

The data experiments observed a reduction to 0.206% of the original source data volume, as an example, from 8.57TB of data to 12.3GB in a digital forensic data subset. The data subsets were then used in Volume 2 to explore processes of quick analysis, and semi-automated information and entity extraction, including a process of value adding to the data subset with open-source information, with positive results.

The proposed digital forensic data reduction and data mining framework provides forensic practitioners with a methodology to guide through the process of digital forensic analysis, allowing for instances where the practitioner can decide whether to undertake full forensic imaging and analysis, or rapidly collect data which is then processed and reviewed in a timely manner. Should the reduction and review process not discover evidence or intelligence of value, the framework provides for this by including an ability to traverse between rapid collection and timely review, and full forensic imaging and analysis. This is not seen in other digital forensic frameworks for analysis.

Adelaide, Australia   Darren Quick
San Antonio, USA   Kim-Kwang Raymond Choo

Acknowledgements

The permission of Elsevier (Chap. 2) and Springer (Chap. 4) for permission to reprint the respective copyrighted material is acknowledged. The views and opinions expressed in this book are those of the authors alone and not the organizations with whom the authors have been associated or supported.

Contents

Abbreviations

$MFT	Windows Master File Table
ACPO	Association of Chief of Police Officers
AD1	AccessData Logical Evidence File
CSV	Comma Separated Value
CTR	X-Ways Logical Image Container
DOCX	Windows Document Format
E01	Encase Physical Evidence Format
EXIF	Exchangeable image file format
EXT3/4	Linux Extended File System
FAT	File Allocation Table
FTK	Forensic Tool Kit
HD	Hard Drive
HFS/+	Apple Hierarchal File System
HTML	Hypertext Markup Language
ICT	Information and Communication Technology
IEF	Internet Evidence Finder
iOS	Apple iPhone Operating System
IP	Internet Protocol
ISO	International Organization for Standardization
IT	Information Technology
JPG	Joint Picture Group
L01	Encase Logical Evidence Format
LT	Laptop
MD5	Message Digest
NIJ	National Institute of Justice
NIST	National Institute of Standards and Technology
NTFS	New Technology File System
OS	Operating System
OSX	Apple Operating System
PC	Personal Computer

PDF	Portable Document Format
PLIST	Property List
PPTX	Microsoft PowerPoint format
RAM	Random Access Memory
RTF	Rich Text Format
SHA	Secure Hash Algorithms
UFED	Forensic Software from Cellebrite for mobile device analysis
URL	Uniform Resource Locator
USB	Universal Serial Bus
VM	Virtual Machine
VMDK	Virtual Machine Disk
XLSX	Microsoft Spreadsheet format
XRY	Forensic software from MSAB for mobile device analysis

Keywords

Big Data · Big Forensic Data · Computer Forensics · Criminal Intelligence
Data Mining · Data Reduction · Data Volume · Digital Evidence
Digital Forensic Analysis · Digital Forensics · Evidence Discovery
Forensic Challenges · Forensic Computer Analysis · Forensic Computing
Forensic Intelligence · Intelligence Analysis · Knowledge Management
Mobile Device Forensic Extracts · Open Source Intelligence · Quick Analysis
Selective Imaging

Chapter 1
Introduction

Digital forensic analysis is the process of identification, preservation, analysis, and presentation of digital evidence in a manner that is legally acceptable (McKemmish 1999). The significant growth in the size of storage media combined with the popularity of digital devices and the decrease in the price of these devices and storage media have led to a major issue affecting the timely process of justice, which is the growing volume of data seized and presented for analysis, often now consisting of many terabytes of data for each investigation.

This increase in digital evidence presented for analysis to digital forensic laboratories has been an issue for many years, leading to lengthy backlogs of work (Justice 2016; Parsonage 2009). This is compounded with the growing size of storage devices (Garfinkel 2010). Digital forensic data holdings consist of large amounts of structured and unstructured data which encompasses a wide variety of file systems, operating systems, software, and user created data, across a range of devices and media types.

Existing forensic software solutions have evolved from the first generation of tools and are now beginning to address scalability issues, but a gap remains in relation to analysis of large and disparate forensic datasets. Processing times are increasing along with the amount of data seized for investigation.

There have been many calls for research to focus on the timely analysis of large datasets (Garfinkel 2010; Richard and Roussev 2006a; Wiles et al. 2007) with solutions explored including the application of data mining techniques to digital forensic data (Beebe and Clark 2005; Palmer 2001) in an endeavour to address the issue of the growing volume of information. The growth in volume and number of devices impacts forensic examinations in many ways, as well as an increase in the backlog of requests, there is also an increase in the length of time to create forensic copies and undertake analysis (Beebe and Clark 2005; Garfinkel 2010). Digital forensic practitioners, especially those in law enforcement agencies, will continue to be under pressure to deliver more with less especially in today's economic landscape.

© The Author(s) 2018
D. Quick and K.-K. R. Choo, *Big Digital Forensic Data*, SpringerBriefs on Cyber Security Systems and Networks, https://doi.org/10.1007/978-981-10-7763-0_1

This gives rise to a variety of needs, including;

- a capacity to triage evidence prior to conducting full analysis,
- a more efficient method of collecting and preserving evidence,
- reduced data storage requirements,
- an ability to conduct a review of information in a timely manner,
- an ability to archive important data,
- an ability to quickly retrieve and review archived data, and
- a source of data to enable a review of current and historical cases for intelligence and knowledge management purposes.

Many policing agencies have dedicated digital forensic sections to undertake analysis of digital evidence. Within these sections the seized devices are forensically copied, processed, analysed, and the results communicated in a format that is able to be presented and understood in a legal environment. Many agencies are struggling to keep up with the growing volume of data presented for analysis, with increasingly larger backlogs of cases (Justice 2016; Parsonage 2009).

Whilst there are a variety of challenges to digital forensic analysis, including encryption, Internet-of-Things (IoT) devices, cloud storage, and anti-forensics, the growth in the volume of data is a major challenge. This is a result of the rapid development of storage technology, including consumer devices and cloud storage. Digital forensic software has evolved from the first generation of tools, but there remains a potential to develop innovative methods to conduct analysis, reducing the time a practitioner spends reviewing superfluous data and focus on data which has a better potential for evidential relevance.

There are a variety of research fields which have potential to impact the volume data challenge, including; Knowledge Discovery, Knowledge Management, Data Mining, and Criminal Intelligence Analysis. Knowledge discovery and knowledge management is an overall process of extracting valuable knowledge from data (Cios and Kurgan 2005). Data mining is a step of the knowledge discovery process and may offer a way to comprehend large volumes of seized data (Fayyad, Piatetsky-Shapiro and Smyth 1996b). Whilst there have been many calls for research in relation to the large volume issue, which include research into whether data mining methodologies can be applied to digital forensic data (Beebe and Clark 2005; Palmer 2001), there is very little published research which progresses this (further discussed in Chap. 2—Literature Review).

Significant gaps remain in relation to applying data mining methodologies to digital forensic data, including a methodology which can be applied to real world data, the benefits which may be observed, and the most appropriate methodology to achieve the desired results including; a reduction in analysis time, a method of archiving and retrieving data, a rapid triage process, and a methodology to gain knowledge from the seized data. It is envisioned that applying the concepts of data mining to digital forensic data will lead to a methodology to assist examiners in analysing the vast volumes of seized data.

Evidential data is the focus when establishing proof, often in a Court environment, whereas 'intelligence' is information which is processed in some form into knowledge which is designed for action (UNODC 2011). In the digital forensic realm there is another major gap relating to the limited use of intelligence gained during digital forensic analysis. Digital forensic intelligence has potentially a large benefit to investigative and other agencies. The current focus of investigations is locating evidence for urgent matters, with little or no time to consider other information which may provide valuable input to current or future investigations. Historically there has been very little discussion of a methodology to utilise the intelligence gained from one digital forensic investigation to assist with other investigations, nor to build a body of knowledge inherent in historical digital forensic cases.

The input of open and closed source intelligence for investigations is anticipated to improve the analysis phase of a digital forensic investigation. For example; information stored on a phone seized for one investigation may provide information to other seemingly unrelated investigations. Without an intelligence or knowledge management process, this information or linkage remains undiscovered. Using knowledge management, intelligence analysis, and data mining methodologies, it is envisioned that a large volume of information could be aggregated into common data holdings, and include the capability for rapid searches to link associated information and assist in investigations, but to enable this, we need a way to collect and process the data in a timely manner, which with the current and increasing volume of data on devices, seems out of reach.

The aim of this book is to outline a framework for digital forensic practitioners to apply data mining and data reduction techniques to digital forensic data to reduce the time to collect data. The focus is to apply data reduction and data mining techniques to a large volume of structured and unstructured data atypical of seized evidential data. Data mining and intelligence analysis techniques are demonstrated with the use of test data and real world (anonymised) data to demonstrate an appropriate methodology which can be applied in real world situations in an effort to address the digital forensic volume data issue.

The use of technology by criminals and/or victims means that data of relevance to an investigation may be located on a variety of devices, or may be virtualised, geographically distributed, or transient. This presents technical and jurisdictional challenges for identification and seizure by law enforcement and national security agencies, which can impede digital forensic investigators and potentially prevent agencies from acquiring digital evidence and forensically analysing digital content in a timely fashion (Taylor et al. 2010). The increasing volume of data is also impacting on timely location of evidence and intelligence on seized devices.

The motivation for conducting research into the growing volume of digital forensic data can be summarised as follows; Electronic devices and storage media, including cloud storage and Internet of Things devices, is increasingly being used by consumers, businesses, and government users to store growing amounts of data, which can be accessed with portable devices, computers, or mobile phones. Criminals are embracing the growth in technology for communication opportunities and the method by which crime is now enabled by technology, such as storing illicit data on portable devices or in cloud file hosting services. Investigations can stall if identification and preservation of potential evidence is not able to be undertaken, or this is not able to be done in a timely manner.

The growing volume of data is contributing to growing backlogs of evidence awaiting analysis, and the increasing time to process and analyse electronic evidence. This can lead to issues with timely identification of offending, and victim identification. There is a need for a process to quickly collect and preserve data in a format which can be rapidly analysed for key evidence or intelligence to progress an investigation in a timely manner.

The next chapter explores published literature focusing on the increase in digital forensic data volume and proposed solutions.

References

Beebe, N., & Clark, J. (2005). Dealing with terabyte data sets in digital investigations. *Advances in Digital Forensics*, pp. 3–16.

Cios, K., & Kurgan, L. (2005). Trends in data mining and knowledge discovery. *Advanced Techniques in Knowledge Discovery and Data Mining*, pp. 1–26.

Fayyad, U., Piatetsky-Shapiro, G., & Smyth, P. (1996). From data mining to knowledge discovery in databases. *AI Magazine, 17*(3), 37.

Garfinkel, S. (2010). Digital forensics research: The next 10 years. *Digital Investigation, 7* (Supplement, no. 0), pp. S64–S73.

Justice, UDo (2016). *Office of the Inspector General. Audit of the federal bureau of investigation's New Jersey regional computer forensic laboratory*, <https://oig.justice.gov/reports/2016/a1611.pdf>.

McKemmish, R. (1999). *What is forensic computing?*

Palmer, G. (2001). A road map for digital forensic research. *Report from the first digital forensic research workshop (DFRWS)*, August 7–8.

Parsonage, H. (2009). *Computer forensics case assessment and triage—some ideas for discussion*, viewed 4 August, <http://computerforensics.parsonage.co.uk/triage/triage.htm>.

Richard, G., & Roussev, V. (2006a). Digital forensics tools: The next generation. *Digital crime and forensic science in cyberspace*, p. 75.

Taylor, M., Haggerty, J., Gresty, D., & Hegarty, R. (2010). Digital evidence in cloud computing systems. *Computer Law & Security Review, 26*(3), 304–308.

UNODC. (2011). *United nations office on drugs and crime—criminal intelligence manual for analysts*. New York, Vienna, Austria: United Nations.

Wiles, J., Alexander, T., Ashlock, S., Ballou, S., Depew, L., Dominguez, G., Ehuan, A., Green, R., Long, J., & Reis, K. (2007). Forensic examination in a terabyte world. *Techno Security's Guide to E-Discovery and Digital Forensics*, Elsevier, pp. 129–146.

Chapter 2
Background and Literature Review

Big Data has been defined as "high-volume, high-velocity and high-variety information assets that demand cost-effective, innovative forms of information processing for enhanced insight and decision making" (Gartner 2013). In the realm of digital forensics, data holdings are increasingly larger, highly complex, consist of large amounts of structured and unstructured data, all intermixed with a variety of file systems, operating systems, devices, and media types. Add to this the increasing use of cloud stored data, and digital forensic practitioners continue to face what has been described as a "coming digital forensic crisis" and the "single largest challenge to conquer" (Garfinkel 2010; Raghavan 2013).

The volume of data has been growing for many years, and whilst a variety of solutions have been proposed, the volume of data continues to increase, and analysis times continue to grow. This is a result of the continuing development of storage technology, including increased storage capacity in consumer devices and cloud storage services, and an increase in the number of devices seized per case. Consequently, this has led to increasing backlogs of evidence awaiting analysis, often many months to years, affecting even the largest digital forensic laboratories (Justice 2015, 2016).

In the current era of organised crime and terrorism activity, there is a need to be able to examine and process large volumes of data in a rapid manner. There has been a variety of research undertaken in relation to the volume challenge. Solutions posed range from data mining, data reduction, increased processing power, distributed processing, artificial intelligence, and other innovative methods. This chapter surveys the published research and the proposed solutions.

The publications were located by searching a range of academic databases, including; IEEE Xplore, ACM Digital Library, Google Scholar, and ScienceDirect

Material presented in this Chapter is based on the following publication:

Quick, D. and K.-K.R. Choo, Impacts of Increasing Volume of Digital Forensic Data: A Survey and Future Research Challenges. Digital Investigation, 2014. 11(4): pp. 273–294 using keywords including; "Digital Forensic Data Volume", "Computer Forensic Volume Problem", "Forensic Data Mining", "Digital Forensic Triage", "Forensic Data Reduction", "Digital Intelligence", "Digital Forensic Growth", and "Digital Forensic Challenges". In addition, all papers published in Digital Investigation: The International Journal of Digital Forensics & Incident Response, and The Journal of Digital Forensics, Security and Law, were examined.

2.1 Background

The increase in the number and volume of digital devices seized and lodged with digital forensic laboratories for analysis is an issue that has been raised over many years. This growth has contributed to lengthy backlogs of work (Gogolin 2010; Parsonage 2009). The significant growth in the size of storage media combined with the popularity of digital devices and the decrease in the price of these devices and storage media has led to a major issue affecting the timely process of justice. There is a growing volume of data seized and presented for analysis, often now consisting of many terabytes of data for individual investigations. This has resulted from;

(a) An increase in the number of devices seized per case.
(b) The number of cases with digital evidence is increasing,
(c) The size of data on each individual item is increasing.

The increasing number of cases and devices seized is further compounded with the growing size of storage devices (Garfinkel 2010; Justice 2016). Existing forensic software solutions have evolved from the first generation of tools and are now beginning to address scalability issues. However, a gap remains in relation to analysis of large and disparate datasets. Every year the volume of data has increased faster than the capability of processors and forensic tools can manage (Roussev et al. 2013).

Processing times have grown with the increase in the amount of data required to be analysed. In the last decade, there have been many calls for research to focus on the timely analysis of large datasets (Garfinkel 2010; Richard and Roussev 2006a; Wiles et al. 2007) including the application of data mining techniques to digital forensic data in an endeavour to address the issue of the growing volume of information (Beebe and Clark 2005; Palmer 2001).

Serious implications relating to increasing backlogs include; reduced sentences for convicted defendants due to the length of time waiting for results of digital forensic analysis, suspects committing suicide whilst waiting for analysis, and suspects denied access to family and children whilst waiting for analysis (Shaw and Browne 2013). In addition, employment can be affected for suspects under investigation for lengthy periods of time, and ongoing difficulties can be experienced by suspects and innocent persons when computers and other devices are seized, for example; the child of a suspect may have school assignments saved on a seized computer, or the partner of a suspect may have all their taxation or business information saved on a laptop.

2.2 Volume of Data

Digital forensics plays a crucial role in society across justice, security and privacy (Casey 2014). Concerns regarding the increasing volume of data to be analysed in a digital forensic examinations have been raised for many years. McKemmish (1999) stated that the rapid increase in the size of storage media is probably the single greatest challenge to digital forensic analysis. In 2001, Palmer published the results of the first Digital Forensic Research Workshop (DFRWS), which included a section from Dr Eugene Spafford discussing various challenges posed to computer forensics and stated, 'Digital technology continues to change rapidly. Terabyte disks and decreasing time to market are but two symptoms that cause investigators difficulty in applying currently available analytical tools' (Palmer 2001).

Sommer (2004) outlined the issues with the increasing data size and number of devices in a legal environment, which is slow to understand the resources and procedures involved, is resulting in methods which do not scale to cope with the increases. Roussev (2004) stated that the vast amounts of disk storage in use by ordinary computer users would soon overwhelm digital forensic investigators. Ferraro and Russell (2004) discussed the increase ubiquitousness of computers, coupled with a notion of a forensic scientist conducting examinations in every computer related crime, leading to demand for forensic science services which outstrips the resources available, and that alternative methods are required. Ferraro and Russell (2004) also outlined the average time digital evidence is retained, stated to be between three and five years or more, and that orders from courts which can mandate impossible or time consuming procedures in evidence handling, can impede timely processing of evidence. Rogers (2004) reported on a study relating to the needs of digital forensic practitioners, and listed the top issues from a survey conducted of 60 respondents indicating that education, training and certification was the most reported issue, and a lack of funding was the least reported issue, with 'technology' and 'data acquisition' in the top four concerns raised by the respondents.

Alink et al. (2006) stated that the volume of data in typical investigations is huge, with modern systems containing hundreds of gigabytes, and large investigations often consist of multiple systems totalling terabytes of data, and in addition, the diversity of data can be overwhelming. Richard and Roussev (2006a) made the observation that most current digital forensic tools are unable to deal with the ever growing size of media, and that new analysis techniques are required, such as automatic categorisation of pictures. Adelstein (2006) stated that the nature of a digital forensic investigation has changed, and the larger disk sizes has resulted in an increase in the time required for collecting a full disk image and then conduct analysis. Furthermore, the nature of digital forensic investigations calls for ongoing technology developments to provide significantly better tools for practitioners (Richard and Roussev 2006b). As an example, Alink et al. (2006) described their prototype system, which displayed timestamp information merged from different tools, highlighting that tools such as EnCase displayed time ordered views of file-system metadata only (and still do).

Wiles et al. (2007) when discussing the challenge of exponential growth in data, specifically the volume and cost to analyse, alluded to forensic practitioners attempting to locate needles in haystacks which becoming larger and more compact. Khan et al. (2007) highlighted that the increasingly larger data volumes, with varying levels of diversity, result in a need for additional resources and additional cost, and that much of the data consists of text, hence text mining methodologies have been proposed to look for patterns.

Case et al. (2008) stated that the 'leading challenge for digital forensic investigations is that of scale.' As the complexity of forensic data increases, forensic tools must adapt to have a broader focus. Rather than concentrating on first-order information, which is merely presented by the current tools in volume to an analyst who then has to understand the information, forensic tools should correlate information from multiple sources, bringing together information generated by a variety of processes (Case et al. 2008). Nance, Hay and Bishop (2009) outlined the results of a brainstorming session from the 2008 Colloquium for Information Systems Security Education addressing the development of a research and education agenda for Digital Forensics, which included the challenge of 'Data Volume', stating it was 'common for digital forensic investigations to be overwhelmed with massive volumes of data', which currently still applies. Riley et al. (2008) examined the common time involved in imaging (for the time) hard drives, and stated that the trend of increasing sized drives presented a challenge to forensic investigators, and with the combination of increasing crime and shortage of examiners there was a large backlog of processing and analysis of evidence, which are still current issues (Justice 2016).

Casey et al. (2009) highlighted that the growing size of storage, the variety of devices, increasing caseloads, and limited resources combined 'to create a crisis for Digital Forensics Laboratories' with many labs having 6–12 month backlogs. Beebe (2009) raised 'Volume and Scalability' as an important strategic direction for research, due to the increasing size of data. Ayers (2009) stated that existing forensic software and tools are inadequate due to the complexity of data and increasingly large volumes of data. Cloud computing was discussed by Biggs and Vidalis (2009) who highlighted that it will likely become a major issue in relation to creation, storage, processing, and distribution of illicit material. Garfinkel et al. (2009a) stated that there is a need for forensic tools which can reconstruct, analyse, cluster, mine, and make sense of the increasing variety and scale of data.

Turnbull et al. (2009) undertook analysis of the figures from the South Australia Police Electronic Crime Section for the period from 1999 to 2008, which showed an average increase of 20% per year growth for the number of requests, and the number of property items was also increasing each year, quantifying the generally observed growth trend. A white paper from Access Data Corporation discussed the issue of the FBI cybercrime labs reported to have large backlogs of cases which delayed investigations, and quoted FBI Executive Assistant Director Stephen Tidwell as saying '[t]he pervasiveness of the Internet has resulted in the dramatic growth of online sexual exploitation of children, resulting in a 2,000% increase in the number of cases opened since 1996' (AccessDataCorporation 2010). It was further stated that 'not only the number of delayed cases that make this an urgent matter. It is the nature of most of these cases that dramatically increases the pressure on computer forensics labs to implement more efficient policies and practices to overcome this issue.'

Biggs and Vidalis (2009) discussed paedophile criminal activity, stating that this crime type accounts for between 70–80% of an investigators workload, and that 'the cloud could prove to be a haven that the paedophile may wish to exploit to fulfil his heinous needs. If data content is not monitored by cloud vendors, then this type of remote storage and relative anonymity of the cloud account holder, may further stretch law enforcement resources beyond breaking point.'

Casey (2010) discussed the pervasiveness of electronic devices in society, in particular the major challenge to keep pace with new developments. Gogolin (2010) surveyed law enforcement agencies in Michigan, USA, and was reported that many agencies reported that 50% of cases have a digital component, and many digital forensic labs had backlogs approaching or exceeding two (2) years, with average caseloads far exceeding average case analysis timeframes.

Garfinkel (2010) discussed the potential challenges of the next decade, and alluded to the growing size of storage devices as 'the coming digital forensic crisis', where due to the growing size of storage devices there will be difficulties in imaging, processing, and assembling terabytes of data into concise reports. The focus of forensic software has been on thoroughness, and minimal development has focussed on performing rapid analysis, i.e. within five-minutes (Garfinkel 2010). However, many commercial forensic software companies have taken steps to address the changing nature of digital evidence and the challenges of the growing volume of data by radically changing the method of storing case files and processing data (AccessDataCorporation 2010; DFI_News 2011). However, this does not necessarily alleviate or address the volume data issue.

Garfinkel (2012a) highlighted the totality of information which makes digital forensic software development distinct from other software development due to; the diversity of data, the volume of data, the need to be using the latest software and operating systems, the pressure on a small group of human practitioners, the time to train new practitioners and programmers (~ 2 years), and unreasonable expectations of clients and judiciary, the so-called "CSI effect." The volume of data is exacerbated by the nature of electronic evidence, in that, top-of-the-line systems are seized and presented for analysis, hence forensic labs need to be equipped with top of the line systems to undertake analysis in a few hours on what has been in use for months or years, concluding that 'we will never get ahead of the performance curve' (Garfinkel 2012a).

Bhoedjang et al. (2012) stated that individual cases often consist of terabytes of data, which could be reviewed by investigators with few technical skills, freeing up technical specialists for higher level tasks, and that 'data volumes and processing times have increased to the point that desktop processing is no longer cost-effective.'

Jones et al. (2012) outlined the increasing demand placed on the Australian New South Wales Police Force (NSWPOL) State Electronic Evidence Branch (SEEB) for digital forensic support, requiring the development of a sampling process to reduce the time spent on analysis of Child Exploitation Material investigations.

Casey et al. (2013) discussed the increase in the number of cases and the increase in the amount of data for each examination, highlighting the need for more efficient tools and processes. Overill et al. (2013) highlighted the growing gap between the demand for services and the capability in law enforcement digital forensic units, and with public sector budget cuts in the current economic climate there 'is no realistic possibility of increasing the level of resourcing to match the ever-increasing demand.' This was supported by Shaw and Browne (2013), who also stated that forensic labs globally are failing to keep pace with demand for services, and that forensic triage is suggested as a method to deal with the "big data" problem. Roussev et al. (2013) examined the process of triage, and highlighted that storage capacity is increasing which will continue to put pressure on forensic tool developers, with a call to focus on real-time processing at the time of imaging, preferably processing is undertaken at the same time as imaging, so the bottleneck is I/O speed, but conclude that 'with current software, keeping up with a commodity SATA HDD at 120 MB/s requires 120–200 cores.'

Quick and Choo (2013b) discussed the increasing use and availability of cloud storage being used by criminals and criminal organisations, further adding to the complexity of the growth in data, and impacting on timely analysis. Alzaabi et al. (2013) discussed the growth in storage capacity and decreasing cost of devices, and whilst tools and techniques assist an investigator, the time and effort to undertake analysis remains a serious challenge. Raghavan (2013) stated that an 'exponential growth of technology has also brought with it some serious challenges for digital forensic research', and the 'volume problem' is the 'single largest challenge to conquer'.

van Baar et al. (2014) discussed the increase in the number of devices and caseload, and outlined the shortcomings of many forensic lab processes, such as having forensic practitioners involved in low level tasks such as network management, system administration, imaging, and other tasks, not necessarily utilising their higher level skill sets for analysis tasks. Breitinger and Roussev (2014) stated that 'one of the biggest challenges facing a digital forensic investigation is coping with the huge number of files that need to be processed' and that *known file filtering* or *hashing* is difficult to maintain as the underlying data within files is altered on a regular basis resulting in reference databases becoming obsolete. Breitinger et al. (2014) reinforced this, stating the time to compare known hash values using current processes is time consuming, and that improved processes can achieve the same result in much faster timeframes.

Vidas et al. (2014) highlighted that the increasing volume of data leading to backlogs of cases within forensic labs, and analysis times of days or weeks, is counterintuitive to the need for fast analysis in many cases. Noel and Peterson (2014) discussed the 'big data problem' which complicates digital investigations, resulting in poor decision making, lost opportunities, failing to discover evidence, and potentially loss of life.

Baggili and Breitinger (2015) discussed the major challenges to cyber forensics, and detailed the lack of suitable test data sources, mentioning the corpus of Garfinkel et al. (2009b) (which was used in this research). They highlighted the potential to use social media data for cyber forensic purposes, and the use of social networks for real-time analysis to solve crimes and identify suspected criminal behaviour.

In the United States Department of Justice (2015) figures from the Audit of the Federal Bureau of Investigation's Philadelphia Regional Computer Forensic Laboratory (RCFL) show that for all Regional Computer Forensic labs, 32.7% of requests are over 6 months old, and 14% of all requests are over 1 year. Considering 'In December 2014, all RCFLs were informed by FBI's Operational Technology Division that service requests that remain open for more than a year are seen as a high risk and could potentially impact the FBI's operational cycle and ability to conduct effective and timely investigations' (Justice 2016). In addition, according to the New Jersey RCFL, the growing backlog is impacted due to 'the storage capacity of the items to be reviewed has dramatically increased over the past three years' (Justice 2016).

Furthermore, 'NJRCFL has made several efforts to manage their case backlog, including bringing on more examiners, implementing policies specific to reducing the backlog that have been approved by the NJRCFL Local Executive Board (LEB), streamlining the examination process, and providing additional advanced training to staff. However, these efforts have not effectively reduced the case backlog' (Justice 2016).

Al Fahdi et al. (2016) examined the increasing volume of data and highlighted the backlog experienced by the United States Department of Justice consisted of 1,566 outstanding cases, of which 57% were between 91 days and over 2 years, and highlighted the focus as shifting from finding every piece of evidence, to intelligence-based searching for sufficient evidence to determine innocence or guilt. They outlined an Automated Evidence Profiler which used Self Organising Map (SOM) based analysis to provide a cluster of notable versus noise files.

Lillis et al. (2016) examined current challenges and future research areas for digital forensics, highlighted the growing use of technology in daily life, and anticipated the number of cases will greatly increase in the future. They highlighted the emerging trends which may contribute to data volume and case backlog issues, which included; Internet of Things (IoT) devices, and cloud computing. They suggested further research in distributed processing, parallel processing, GPU multi-threading, Digital Forensics as a Service (DFaaS), Field Programmable Gate Arrays (FPGA), and the application of latest research to digital forensics, such as Information Retrieval, event timeline reconstruction, and unstructured text retrieval.

2.3   Growth of Media

In the previous section the many digital forensic papers discussing the problem of increasing volumes of data and devices were outlined. In this section, the focus relates to growth of media.

Moore's Law is the observation of an average doubling of the number of transistors on an integrated circuit every 18–24 months, which assists in predicting development of computer technology (Wiles et al. 2007). Kryder (as discussed in Walter 2005) made the observation that in the space of 15 years, the storage density of hard disks had increased 1,000 fold, from 100 million bits per square inch in 1990–2005 when 110 gigabit drives were released by Seagate. Kryders Law equates to storage density of hard drives doubling every 12 months, holding true since 1995 (Wiles et al. 2007). The doubling of hard drive size is about twice the pace of Moore's Law (Coughlin 2001). This highlights that storage capacity is doubling roughly every year and the capacity to process data is doubling every 18–24 months, leading to a potential growing gap in the capability to process data.

Roussev and Richard (2004) discussed the growth in CPU speeds in comparison with I/O transfer speeds, and observe that I/O speeds have not kept up with CPU speeds, and if they had, 'it would take about the same amount of time to image a 20 GB drive as it would to image a 200 GB drive' (at the time), and that 'anybody who has tried a similar experiment knows that this is absolutely not the case.' Roussev et al. (2013) undertook further study in relation to real-time processing of hard drive data, and concluded that the volume of data is increasing exponentially, and the amount of processing required was increasing faster than the capability of workstations and many forensic tools.

In 1999, a 10 GB hard drive was considered a large amount of data (McKemmish 1999). Culley (2003) stated that it was not uncommon for computer evidence to consist of a terabyte or more in 2003. Alink et al. (2006) described testing of a prototype system on forensic images ranging from 40 to 240 GB. Wiles et al. (2007) stated that as companies and government agencies are storing petabytes of data, it is possible that large digital forensic cases may approach this volume of data. Pringle and Sutherland (2008) stated that in 2007 it took approximately 24 h to image a 500 GB hard drive. When Riley et al. (2008) reviewed the imaging times for common hard drives, they used 80, 120, and 250 GB hard disk drives, with imaging times ranging from 30 min to nearly 2 h. Zimmerman (2013) also conducted testing of imaging times, using a 1 TB hard drive for a range of testing, with time ranging from 2.5 to 5.5 h.

Craiger et al. (2005) reported on the volume of data examined by the United States Federal Bureau of Investigation (FBI) Computer Analysis Response Team (CART) for the Years 1999–2003, as presented to the 14th INTERPOL Forensic Science Symposium, and calculated the number of cases increasing threefold, and the volume of data increasing by forty-six times, stated to be many times the volume of data in the largest library on Earth, the United States Library of Congress. Averaging the number of cases with the data burden (Table 2.1) shows

Table 2.1   FBI CART examinations (INTERPOL 2004)

US (Fiscal year)	1999	2000	2001	2002	2003
Caseload	2084	3,591	5,166	5,924	6,546
Data burden (TB)	17	39	119	358	782
Average case size (GB)	8	11	23	60	119

Table 2.2   FBI RCFL annual reports 2003–2016 (FBI_RCFL 2003–2016)

US fiscal year	Service requests received	Examinations conducted	TB processed	Average case size (GB)
2003	1,444	987	82	83
2004	1,548	1,304	229	176
2005	3,434	2,977	457	154
2006	4,214	3,633	916	252
2007	4,567	4,634	1,288	278
2008	5,057	4,524	1,756	388
2009	5,616	6,016	2,334	388
2010	5,985	6,564	3,086	470
2011	6,318	7,629	4,263	559
2012	5,060	8,566	5,986	699
2013	6,040	7,273	5,973	821
2014	6,994	6,322	5,060	800
2015	6,321	5,897	5,276	895
2016	5,939	5,229	5,667	1084
Total	68,537	71,555	42,373	

an increase in average per-case size from 8 GB in FY1999 to 119 GB in FY2003. In 2002 it was stated that fifty percent of the cases opened by the FBI involved a computer (Peisert et al. 2008). In 2010, fifty percent (50%) of cases in the Michigan, USA area involved digital evidence (Gogolin 2010).

In a further effort to assess the growth in digital forensic data volume, information from the FBI Regional Computer Forensic Laboratory (RCFL) Annual Reports from Fiscal Year (FY) 2003–2016 was reviewed. The data and figures in the reports was compiled and is summarised in Table 2.2 (FBI_RCFL 2003–2012). The figures show a growth in the total volume of data, from 82 Terabytes (TB) in 2003 to 5,986 TB (5.8 Petabytes) in 2012, an overall increase of an average of 67% per annum. In FY 2003, the average size for a case was approximately 83 GB, which grew to approximately 1,084 GB in FY 2016, an average increase of 25% per annum per case. In addition, the US Department for Homeland Security reportedly processed 5.2 PB of data in fiscal year 2014, and observed a 4,000% increase in the volume of data presented between 2004 and 2012 (Rockwell 2015).

Roussev et al. (2013) outlined the acquisition rates based on maximum sustained throughput of hard drives to approximate that, in 2003 a 200 GB hard drive should take about one hour to image at 58 MB/s, and in 2013 a 3 TB hard drive to take almost seven hours at 123 MB/s, but they then stated that in reality a 3 TB hard drive actually took over 11 h to image, at the time. They demonstrated the increase in imaging and processing times, and concluded that this will continue as I/O improvements do not keep pace with volume increases, and that current workstation hardware does not offer enough processing power to keep up with a SATA hard drive.

The International Data Corporation stated that the world's volume of data doubles every 18 months, and the cost of storage has fallen; for example, a 2 terabyte (TB) hard drive in 2010 cost the same as an 18 gigabyte (GB) hard drive in 1998 (Wong 2010). A single megabyte (MB) of hard drive storage in 1956 was US $10,000, which dropped to US$300 by 1983, US$0.07 in 1998, and US$0.0005 in 2010, (with a 250 GB drive costing $125) (Growchowski 1998; Wong 2010). According to PC World, hard disk drives, which were introduced in 1956, took 35 years to reach one gigabyte, 14 more years to reach 500 GB, and only two more years to double to one terabyte (Reyes et al. 2007).

Sommer (2004) wrote that a typical retail PC at that time contained an 80 GB hard disk drive, which was an increase from 20 GB the previous year. In the same year, Roussev and Richard (2004) stated that a 200 GB hard disk cost approximately $165, and that a terabyte-class storage system cost under $1000. When Turner (2005) outlined a method of selective imaging to deal with the so-called 'imminent doomsday' relating to the volume of data, a single hard disk drive at that time was stated to be 'in excess of 350 GB'. In 2008, 2 TB of storage was available for under $500 (Riley et al. 2008). In 2014, 4 TB hard drives were available for less than US$150 (Walmart 2014). Casey stated that 200 GB is capable of storing about 4,000,000 pictures. Extrapolating this, 4 TB, at the time, would be capable of storing 80 million pictures, an enormous volume of pictures for an examiner to view and classify. In addition, it was possible to store 120,000 min of compressed video on a 4 TB hard drive (Bell 2013). To put that into more comprehensible numbers, this equated to 2000 h, or 83 days' worth of video, which for an examiner (working 9 am–5 pm Monday to Friday) would take approximately 50 weeks to play every video file in full.

Data from the South Australia Police (SAPOL) Electronic Crime Section (ECS) for 2013 indicated cases with hard drive sizes of 1–2 TB for single drives, with some up to 4 TB, and some computers contained half a dozen terabyte size hard drives in a RAID configuration. The majority of cases had multiple computers, storage media, and portable devices per investigation, often comprised many terabytes of data in total (Authors' compilation). This raises questions regarding hard drive and storage media sizes over the last 10 years in comparison with the sizes of hard drives seized for digital forensic analysis, and the average number of devices per investigation over this period of time. It is, perhaps, timely to revisit the work of Turnbull et al. (2009), with updated data, to determine the data volume trend since 2009. Table 2.3 compiles the information discussed in this

Table 2.3 Timeline of developments of computers and hard drives

Year	HDD	FBI	FileSystem & USB	OS	Processor	PC's[i]
1956	RAMAC 1MB cost $10k					
~	~					
1977						Apple][(4KB RAM) CBM PET
1980	IBM 1GB HDD for $40k		FAT12			
1981	5MB Seagate HDD			MSDOS	IBM Acorn	VIC20 (5KB RAM)
1982					286	C64 (64KB RAM)
1983						
1984						Apple Macintosh (128KB RAM)
1985					386	Amiga 1000 (256KB RAM)
1986	IDE HD			MS Windows		
1987	20MB/40MB		FAT16			
1988	16MB SSD					Amiga 500 (512 KB RAM)
1989					486	
1990	40MB 3,500 RPM			Windows 3.1		Amiga 3000 (2MB RAM)
1991	1GB 20MB SSD			Linux kernal		Apple PowerBook (2MB RAM)
1992	2.1GB		FAT32			Amiga 4000 (2MB RAM)
1993					Pentium	
1994			NTFS	Linux 1.0		
1995	3.2GB 5,400 RPM			Windows 95		Apple PowerMac (8MB RAM)
1996				Linux 2.0		Apple PowerBook (16MB RAM)
1997	16.8GB		USB1.1		Pentium II	
1998	18GB HDD	(GB)		Windows 98		Apple iMac (32MB RAM)
1999		8			Pentium III	Apple iBook (32MB RAM)
2000		11	USB2		Pentium 4	
2001		23		Windows XP	Xeon	Apple OSX
2002	40GB 7,200 RPM	60				
2003	512MB SSD	119		AMD 64 bit ... Pentium M		
2004	SATA HD	176		Ubuntu Linux		Apple iBook G4 (512MB RAM)
2005	500GB HDD 32GB SSD	154		OpenSUSE Linux		Apple iMac G5 (256MB RAM)
2006	750GB	252		Windows Vista		Apple MacBook Pro (1GB RAM)
2007	1TB 320GB SSD	278				Apple Mac Pro (Intel) (2GB RAM)
2008	1.5TB	388	USB3			Apple Mac Pro (3GB RAM)
2009	2TB	388	SATA3	MS Windows 7		
2010	1TB SSD	470			2nd Gen Intel	Apple iPad
2011	4TB	559		Linux 3.0		
2012		699		Windows 8	3rd Gen Intel	Apple Mac Pro (8GB RAM)
2013	5TB	821	USB3.1		4th Gen Intel	
2014	6TB	800	USB-C			Apple Mac Pro Gen 2 (16GB)
2015	8TB 16TB SSD	895		Windows 10 Linux 4.0		
2016	10TB 60TB SSD	1084			6th Gen Intel	
2017	12TB				7th Gen Intel	
2018	16TB				8th Gen Intel	Apple Mac Pro Gen 3 (announced)

section in a timeline format, highlighting the average sizes of hard disk drives, the average memory (RAM) in consumer computers, milestones for technology such as USB, IDE, SATA, Windows operating systems, Intel processors, and includes the FBI CART and RCFL average case volumes (from Tables 2.1 and 2.2).

Figure 2.1 charts the general trend in the volume of Hard Drives with the growth in RAM of Apple Mac Pro computers and the average case size for the FBI CART and RCFL from Tables 2.1, 2.2 and 2.3. A logarithmic scale base 2 is used as the scale of the increase in hard drive size is greater than the scale of the RAM and FBI volumes, skewing the chart when a standard scale is used.

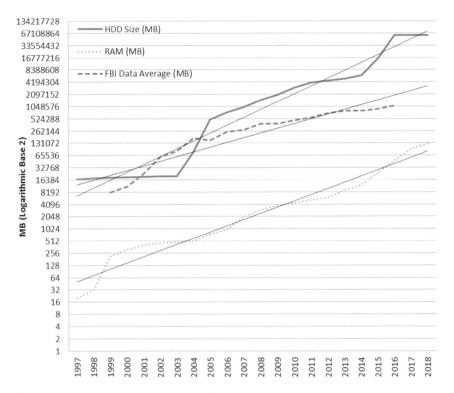

Fig. 2.1 General trend in HDD, RAM, and FBI case size (1997–2014)

2.4 Processing Time

In relation to processing the imaged forensic data, Roussev and Richard (2004) outlined processing and indexing timeframes using FTK 1.43a compared with a prototype distributed system over a six gigabyte (6 GB) forensic image (which would now be considered quite small) and discussed timeframes of about two hours when using FTK 1.43a, and over four days for an 80 GB hard disk drive, using a 'high-end' Windows XP machine consisting of a 3 GHz Pentium4 processor with 2 GB of RAM. Even at the time, when extrapolating these timeframes, the processing time becomes a major bottleneck to investigations.

Riley et al. (2008) reported on research conducted in regard to indexing an 80 GB hard drive, stated at the time to take more than four days, and concluded that the time to index 2 TB of data would be over two months, although they stated the system resources would fail before it could complete. At the time of writing (September 2016), processing and indexing this volume of data is possible with current forensic tools, and, whilst time consuming, is not too onerous. However, there is a lack of current or historical research examining processing times of common amounts of data using common processing solutions. SAPOL ECS figures (and the authors' personal experience) indicate examiners often have many terabytes of data for a single investigation, which is spread over a multitude of devices, with various file and operating systems (Authors compilation). The total time to image and process the media in these cases is lengthy. The capability of a human examiner to understand the massive volume of data is not able to keep pace with the ability to gather and store the data (Fayyad et al. 1996b). Hence, new techniques are required in relation to undertaking digital forensic copying and digital forensic analysis.

Leimich et al. (2016) discussed imaging of Hadoop File system HDFS and the observation that even when writing simultaneously to four external devices with a transfer rate of 6 GB/min, it would take 28 days to image one petabyte of data, and with further time to make a copy for analysis purposes, would be 56 days to acquire and copy one petabyte of data (also see Fowler 2012).

In general, digital evidence must be relevant and credible, and the collection, fusion and correlation of disparate data is vital to digital investigations (Palmer 2002). The challenges do not only relate to processing the volume of data in a timely manner, but also copying and storing increasingly larger volumes of information (McKemmish 1999). Mobile portable devices, such as mobile phones and tablets, also complicate forensic examinations. Mobile phones are reported to be a particular problem due to the large variety of manufacturers, models, and operating systems, making it difficult to gather a full physical copy of data, and rely on logical access to collect data (Reyes et al. 2007). The pervasiveness of these mobile devices results in many criminal and civil investigations having electronic evidence.

McKemmish (1999) stated that as the size of hard drives increases, so too does the amount of data stored, including multimedia, and the demand for increasing storage is also fuelled by the Internet and access to media content to the average user. Palmer (2002) discussed challenges to digital forensic analysis including the trend towards disparate information, with networked systems and devices hosting data, potentially anywhere in the world. Wiles et al. (2007) observed that as the size of media increases, users are storing more, including; every email, document, spreadsheet, picture and video they have, and as storage is easily purchased and inexpensive, there is little need to organize their data. Cloud stored data poses difficulties to forensic analysis, as there can be large volumes of data hosted in disparate locations (Quick et al. 2014).

2.5 Proposed Solutions

Spafford (as cited in Palmer 2001) listed data mining as a field of specialty which may assist in digital forensic analysis. Beebe (2009) also stated that the use of data mining techniques may be another solution to the volume challenge, and also that data mining has the potential to locate trends and information that may otherwise be undetected by human observation. Beebe also raised a list of topics for further research, including;

- a method for subset collection,
- how data mining research can be extended to digital forensics,
- what adaptions are required to apply data mining to forensic data sets, and
- whether link analysis techniques be applied to digital forensic data (Beebe 2009).

2.5.1 Data Mining

Data mining is a process of 'extracting useful information from large data sets or databases' and utilises various types of information processing, including; statistics, machine learning, data management, pattern recognition, and artificial intelligence. Data mining arose from the interest in the growing volume of large databases, in diverse business areas, such as retail transaction data, credit card use records, telephone call data, and government statistics (Hand et al. 2001). Data mining methodologies have been applied to security and intrusion detection data, an associated field to digital forensics, to discover patterns of user behaviour to recognise anomalies and intrusions (Lee and Stolfo 2000). Data mining has also been used in a variety of areas with large data sets, and is useful to summarise incomplete data, and can be used to potentially identify user behaviour to develop user profiles (Abraham 2006). There is potential to apply data mining techniques to digital forensic data to assist with the data volume challenge, and for knowledge and intelligence discovery purposes.

Brown et al. (2005) developed a process of mining forensic data, with the focus on picture analysis and detecting and filtering partially clothed persons from other pictures using colour space and vector composition. In conjunction with other filtering systems, this process can greatly reduce the amount of information a practitioner must sift through. Huang et al. (2010) outlined a framework using ontology matching and machine learning to gather knowledge from large volumes of digital evidence by matching conceptual models to enable data mining and knowledge discovery. They proposed the use of a Bayesian Networks approach, but stated that whilst rule based algorithms are fast, there is a potential to miss information (Huang et al. 2010). Both offer solutions, but apply only to small aspects of the overall digital forensic analysis process, and do not offer comprehensive methodology which can be applied across the whole range of information and evidence required to be analysed.

Data mining has the potential to benefit digital forensics in relation to reducing the processing time, improving the information quality, reducing the cost of analysis, and improving the ability to discover patterns which may otherwise remain unknown (Beebe and Clark 2005). However, there are limitations, as raised by Shannon (2004) in relation to missing important information. Beebe and Clark (2005) also stated that additional limitations relate to the untested nature of applying data mining techniques to forensic data, and the general lack of understanding of

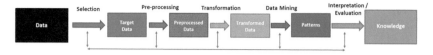

Fig. 2.2 Overview of the steps constituting the KDD process (Adapted from Fayyad et al. 1996b)

data mining techniques in the field of digital forensics. To address the limitations, Beeb and Clark (2005) highlighted a need to increase the awareness of data mining techniques in the digital forensic community, train examiners in data mining techniques, and to create a framework for using data mining techniques in examinations, calling for active research to extend data mining to digital forensics and investigations (Beebe and Clark (2005).

The process of understanding data is known by a variety of names, such as; data mining, 'knowledge extraction, information discovery, information harvesting, data archaeology, and data pattern processing' (Fayyad et al. 1996a, b). Data mining is a step in the process of Knowledge Discovery in Databases (KDD) which is a process of extracting useful information from the growing volume of digital data, which is used in a variety of fields, such as; business, manufacturing, scientific, and personal information (Fayyad et al. 1996b). KDD is a process of understanding data, and the methods and techniques to do this, which are addressed by mapping low-level data which is too large to easily understand, using specific data mining methods relating to pattern discovery and extraction. The nine-step process of KDD, namely: (1) learning the domain, (2) creating a target dataset, (3) data cleaning and pre-processing, (4) data reduction and projection, (5) choosing the function of data mining, (6) choosing the data mining algorithm, (7) data mining, (8) interpretation, and (9) using the knowledge (Fayyad et al. 1996a), is visualised in Fig. 2.2.

The knowledge discovery (KD) process is aimed at identifying potentially useful patterns from large collections of data, and includes data mining as a step (Cios and Kurgan 2005). KD is the overall process of preparing, mining, verifying, and applying the discovered knowledge from data. There are a variety of data mining algorithms with different techniques suited to different problems, and a variety of methods to determine the appropriate algorithm to solve problems (Fayyad et al. 1996a). The general approach of data mining can be for predictive and/or descriptive reasons, or a combination of both (Fayyad et al. 1996a). In addition, the technique of 'Content Retrieval' deals with extracting information from complex, semi-structured, or unstructured data (Hand et al. 2001). Content retrieval techniques are usually applied to the domain of textual data, multimedia data, Internet data, spatial data, time-series or sequential data, and complex data (Beebe and Clark 2005). This has, perhaps, the most promise in relation to digital forensic data.

Hearst (1999) discussed the process of extracting meaning from large text collections, which can be difficult to decipher, and outlined the application of information access and corpus based computational linguistics to enable text data mining. Digital forensic evidence can consist of structured and unstructured data, noisy and clean, and from a variety of sources (Beebe and Clark 2005). Hence, a variety of data mining techniques may be required. A text mining process across an information repository also has potential to assist examiners (Weiser et al. 2006).

Hand et al. (2001) discussed the various methods of predictive, descriptive, and content retrieval data mining. All three methods have potential application in relation to the data mining of digital forensic data holdings, and content retrieval is, perhaps, the most promising due to the variety of structured and unstructured data common to digital forensic evidence. Beebe and Clark (2005) stated that descriptive data modelling is likely to have limited application in digital forensic analysis due to issues around data loss, but that the process may have application in relation to internal investigations and military investigations.

Content retrieval, also known as text mining or information retrieval, is well researched, due to the recent increase in demand for business intelligence, and the increase in data availability (Beebe and Clark 2005). Shannon (2004) outlined a content mining technique called Forensic Relative Strength Scoring (FRSS) in which ASCII proportionality and entropy calculation was used to create a value for text and data, and this was used to filter the data to locate information which can be of benefit to an examiner. However, Shannon (2004) stated that there is a chance that the FRSS process will miss important information, and was intended to be a guide, and not to be depended on to locate information. Hence, there are potential issues in relation to using this technique when applied in a legal environment. Noel and Peterson (2014) proposed the use of natural language processing method of Latent Dirichlet Allocation (LDA) to process user data within forensic data holdings. However, in testing they concluded that the LDA process is much slower than a regular expression (regex) search, with an example of a regex search taking 1 min in comparison with the LDA process taking over 8 h. In a situation where a life is at risk, the large difference in time to process may be hazardous.

Business analytics is a process of designing the needs of data analysis into business systems from the outset, specifically including and addressing the areas of; data collection, data generation, data storage, and integration from multiple sources (Kohavi et al. 2002). This field provides methods to implement data analysis within entire business systems, and aspects of this may have application in the overall setup of a digital forensic analysis environment. However, as digital forensic analysis has differing requirements to the usual fields that these techniques are applied to, there is a need for specific research to address the unique issues applicable to forensic analysis. The steps of the business analytics process align to the processes described for KD, KDD, Intelligence Analysis, and Digital Forensics. The process of business analytics is visualised in Fig. 2.3.

Data mining methodologies can assist with analysis of digital forensic data, and the sub phases of data surveying, extraction, and examination (Beebe and Clark 2005). Descriptive modelling can be used to profile use and activity during the initial data survey phase. Classification techniques can be used to reduce the volume of data to be analysed, and entity extraction techniques, content retrieval, and link analysis follow this (Beebe and Clark 2005). Link analysis can be used to visualise associations amongst entities identified in the content retrieval stage. The crime data analysis phase can be broken up into sub-phases of transformation,

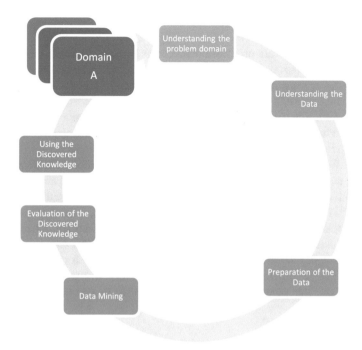

Fig. 2.3 Business analytics (Adapted from Kohavi et al. 2002)

detection, and visualisation. During the transformation stage, data from the various disparate sources is converted to a common format to develop an understanding of the data. Next, predictive mining techniques can be used to identify clusters or groups of entities, associations, and networks, using visualisation techniques to display and analyse the information (Beebe and Clark 2005).

Data mining processes have potential application to assist forensic examiners. However, an overall method to apply this to forensic examinations remains a gap. Okolica et al. (2007) discussed the use of the Author-Topic model to identify the interests of a person from email text in an effort to identify insider threats. Iqbal et al. (2008) outlined a method for applying data mining techniques to email text to identify authors in an endeavour to locate fraudulent messages. Iqbal et al. (2010) built on this work to identify writing styles in an email collection.

Halboob et al. (2015) proposed a framework for digital forensic analysis which involved the use of a data warehouse, but the proposed process relied on an investigator to review and select relevant evidence, which can be time consuming and is quite possible to miss intelligence and evidential data due to human error.

Parashar et al. (2015) proposed a framework for a review of mobile applications using cloud-based forensic analysis using data mining with a view to locate malware in Android Apps. Whilst this process used a data mining approach, it is not aimed at the data volume issue, or the process of digital forensic analysis.

Quintana et al. (2015) discussed the use of data mining recommender systems using large multimedia data collections as applied to digital forensic investigations. Recommender systems are used for media content applications, i.e. recommending media and content to users from a large collection, and they proposed that these recommender systems may have application for digital forensic investigation, and are developing a system for testing.

Hicks et al. (2016) explored the application of web mining techniques to unstructured text found in digital forensic data. They proposed a new algorithm for ranking unstructured text using Google PageRank as the focus.

Casey (2014) commented that; as the volume of data increases, more attention is placed on research using big data solutions and visualisation techniques. Garfinkel (2012a) advocated that the difficulty in applying "big data" solutions to digital forensic data is due to the diverse nature of forensic data, such that solutions for other problems often consist of large amounts of data which can be reduced and locally processed, and that state based agencies do not have the budget or personnel to utilise the data processing methods of large world-renowned physics labs. Hence data mining alone may not provide a complete solution to the growing volume of digital forensic data, and other methods may need to be combined for an overall solution.

2.5.2 Data Reduction and Subsets

Data reduction is a method used in data mining and other analytics systems to reduce the volume of data required to be analysed. There are a variety of methods available for reducing data, including: Features Reduction, Entropy Measure, Principal Component Analysis, Values Reduction, and Cases Reduction (Kantardzic 2011). An objective of data preparation is to produce a primed data set which is of the best use for analysis, the original data is least altered, and is best enhanced for the purpose of the practitioner (Pyle 1999).

Data reduction is a process of "finding useful features to represent the data depending on the goal of the task" (Fayyad et al. 1996c). The goal of digital forensic analysis is to locate evidence or intelligence regarding a crime or breach of policy; therefore, there is a need to collect and analyse the data which will enable this.

Data reduction is a step prior to data mining, and in this era of vast data volumes seized for analysis, the application of this could have potential in digital forensic examinations. Spafford (as cited in Palmer 2001) stated that there is a need to understand what information needs to be collected to provide an accurate analysis for a particular circumstance. This alluded to a process of not collecting everything, but to focus collection of that which will provide an accurate analysis. ACPO (2006) also supported this, advising that 'partial or selective file copying may be considered as an alternative in certain circumstances e.g. when the amount of data to be imaged makes this impracticable. However, investigators should be careful to ensure that all relevant evidence is captured if this approach is adopted.'

Grier and Richard (2015) proposed a method of selective imaging and outlined a process of scanning a hard drive for files and data of high forensic value using sifting profiles tailored for specific investigations, including the involvement of human-in-the-loop to decide what is relevant and selected for collection. This process is akin to that of Sniper Forensics (Greiner 2009), with similar concerns relating to case-type specific filters only collecting case-type related data and information which potentially miss evidence of other criminality. As an example, focussing on financial files and data in a fraud investigation may miss pictures and videos relating to child exploitation. In addition, the process is outlined in relation to the collection stage, whereas there are occasions when a full forensic image is available, but processing and reviewing a full forensic image is not able to be undertaken in a timely manner, necessitating a need for a method to reduce the volume of data for processing purposes rather than collection purposes.

Culley (2003) raised the issue of the efficiency of imaging entire hard drives, but stated that full imaging remained the desirable and thorough option at that time. Now that larger datasets are becoming the norm (and often referred to as 'Big Data'), and logical imaging is implemented in commercial forensic analysis software, it is timely to consider the process of collecting targeted data within the larger volume of evidence and the potential time and resource savings this can provide. Pollitt (2013) mentioned "sufficiency of examination", stated to be coined by Mike Phelan, late Director of DEA, alluding to doing enough examination to answer the required questions, and no more. Collecting a data subset is potentially easily implemented, with minimal changes to current systems and procedures, and can be undertaken in a forensically sound manner when abiding with common forensic principles (e.g., ACPO 2006 or NIJ 2004).

With the volume of data increasing as discussed, one method to address this is to only image and index selected files, and to exclude files and data which do not assist an examiner. There is a potential to reduce time and resource requirements by making decisions prior to imaging to only examine that which may be relevant. Ferraro and Russell (2004) stated that, in relation to child exploitation image investigations, it should be sufficient to locate the necessary evidence to support a criminal investigation and prosecution, without the need for a full forensic examination for all cases.

Turner (2005, 2006) discussed selective imaging and "Digital Evidence Bags" as a method to store a variety of digital evidence whilst retaining information relating to the source and location of the data subset. Schatz and Clark (2006) in building on this, proposed the concept of a "Sealed Digital Evidence Bag", providing for referencing between evidence bags to build a corpus of evidence, using the Resource Description Framework (RDF) to annotate information contained within datasets.

Alzaabi et al. (2013) described the use of RDF when applied to data obtained from Android devices and the use of an ontology based system to interpret data traces for analysts. Turnbull and Randhawa (2015) discussed the rise in devices and data volume leading to increases in digital forensic workloads, and they proposed a method to extract 'events' from forensic artefacts, such as system events and user events, using Resource Descriptive Framework (RDF) as an ontology basis to build a snapshot of use of a device. Their proposed process is being further developed and tested.

Commercial forensic software such as Guidance Software EnCase and AccessData Forensic Tool Kit currently provide a capability to selectively imaging files to support the collection of subset data into logical evidence files.

Garfinkel (2012b) discussed Digital Forensics XML (DFXML) as a method to store common forensic information as a generic data store for a range of tools, enabling parsed data to be stored in a common format to enable better analysis across a variety of information types. XIRAF (XML Information Retrieval Approach to digital forensics) used XML as a format to store the output of a range of forensic tools (Alink et al. 2006). It is also stated that data reduction is a key approach with XIRAF, along with caching, parallel processing, and close interaction with users (Bhoedjang et al. 2012).

The process of selecting which files to image can be a challenge (Beebe 2009). Many child exploitation investigations require additional and thorough analysis to determine what actions a user has undertaken with specific files. In these cases, a variety of other files become important, such as Link files, Prefetch files, Windows Registry files, and other structured and unstructured data. Some of this information may be in unallocated space and, hence, access to the full image may still be necessary. An examiner could be criticised if potential evidence has been discarded due to the perceived cost in time and resources of making a full forensic image, and conducting thorough analysis. There is still a great opportunity for the process of data subsets and selective imaging (see Chap. 4). Whilst in some instances this does not entirely replace the need for full analysis, a process of data reduction can serve to enable a rapid initial analysis.

Child exploitation investigations are one of the most investigated categories for digital forensic analysis (Turnbull et al. 2009). These investigations have a general focus towards pictures, videos, internet chat, and browser history. With these investigation types, a question is raised whereby; "Is it necessary to image entire hard drives, especially when these drives are in the multi terabytes and can often contain known data of little relevance to the investigation (e.g. movie files, television shows, and music)?". Richard and Roussev (2006b) discussed a process of selective imaging by removing known files at the imaging stage, and also only collecting pictures when dealing with a child exploitation investigation. However, there are additional files that have potential evidence for these investigation types, which should be collected and analysed. In some investigations an examiner may need to undertake analysis of a full forensic image if evidence is not located in the subset collected, for example; picture files within an encrypted or compressed file may be missed in a subset collection methodology.

Kenneally and Brown (2005) discussed a 'Risk Sensitive Collection Methodology' whereby selected artefacts are extracted during the initial collection stage, and can be applied to the collection stage when examining so-called 'dead' systems, and also live system extractions. This approach was designed to reduce costs in relation to time and resources, and also evidence storage requirements (Kenneally and Brown 2005). In addition, Kenneally and Brown (2005) further explained a process of selective imaging to address risks associated with collecting full forensic images from large hard drives, which are stated to be primarily the cost in time and resources. This was done by selecting data to image at the collection stage. Legal standards of reasonableness and relevance were raised to address concerns in not undertaking analysis of a full forensic image. However, it could be argued that if the difference relates to hours or days, in a criminal or civil investigation (which can potentially take many months or years) it could be deemed reasonable to take a full bit-for-bit image, and conduct analysis with all available and potentially relevant data where appropriate.

Garfinkel (2009a) introduced Forensic Feature Extraction (FFE) and Cross Drive Analysis (CDA) methods. FFE is outlined as a focus on particular information, such as; email addresses, message information, date and time information, cookies, social security and credit card numbers (Garfinkel 2006a). Information from a scan of a drive would be stored for analysis and comparison. However, by interpreting the data and not storing the original, there may be instances where new techniques cannot be applied to the original data. There have been developments in recent years whereby new information is able to be extracted from data holdings that were previously unknown. For example, Windows Registry analysis methodologies include new areas for locating information (Carvey 2011; Mee et al. 2006). Hence, there is value to storing and retaining original files and the contained data within a logical evidence file to allow for subsequent processing in the future, as and when new tools and processes are developed.

CDA is a process of forensic analysis of data that spans multiple drives or data sources. According to Garfinkel (2006a), the process of CDA used the features extracted using FFE to make cross drive analysis more efficient and to focus forensic analysis on particular features. Future work included extending the process with more accurate scores between drives, improved ability to work with large data sets, better feature extractors, and language–aware systems. It was concluded that whilst automated tools would be preferable, it is likely to be easier to initially create interactive tools for practitioners to drive that also undertake pre-processing functions.

FFE and CDA involved automatically gathering evidence and intelligence from disparate forensic datasets (Garfinkel 2006a). With the growth in the volume of digital forensic data, cross device analysis is problematic when attempting to review and analyse more than a few full forensic images of hard drives and other media, running into issues in relation to collection and processing time, especially timely searching and analysis with the ever growing velocity, variety, and volume of data.

CDA and FFE were extended with the development of bulk_extractor software for the purposes of digital media triage and bulk data analysis (Garfinkel 2013). This extended FFE to scan a disk image or stream of data, including a parallel processing capability, with a focus on credit card numbers, email addresses, URLs, JPG EXIF headers, GPS coordinates, JSON, KML, prefetch files, wordlist, expands compressed files, and other parsers. Histogram analysis is also used to determine common email addresses and search terms.

Greiner (2009) referred to the searching of entire forensic datasets as akin to 'shotgun forensics', i.e. imaging everything and looking for relevant information, and that a more appropriate approach is 'sniper forensics', whereby a targeted approach focussing on pertinent information is used, with investigators knowing what to look for, and when the information is found to stop looking. However, in some investigations, there is a chance that information in relation to other offending may be discovered whilst undertaking analysis, and crucial information may be missed by focussing on specific information based on an investigation typology. As an example, in a child exploitation investigation, an examiner may locate Internet chat which provides evidence of "making a child amenable". If the focus is only on the possession of pictures or other media, then this potential offending may be missed, and a child may remain at risk. Hence, the process of data reduction should collect all data that may provide information without necessarily basing this on a type of suspected offending.

Beebe (2009) posed a solution to the volume and scalability challenge as 'selective digital forensic acquisition', or identifying subsets of data for imaging rather than imaging entire physical devices. However, Beebe (2009) also stated that selective acquisition should include allocated and unallocated space, but does not allude to the reasoning behind this statement, stating that research was needed to determine the process of identifying which files are necessary to acquire. Richard and Roussev (2006a) discussed selective imaging, but stated that the number of potentially excluded files may be small, and hence not achieve much of a reduction in volume and, hence, other approaches should be examined.

Casey et al. (2013) proposed a processing method whereby data is fed simultaneously to separate extraction operations, whilst a full forensic image is taken, hence providing the ability to image, verify, extract and carve with a 32% increase in time over standard imaging. They also proposed to store extracted information in standardised database format such as XML and SQLite. Whilst this potentially serves the need to undertake analysis of the information, there is still a need to undertake a full forensic image, resulting in this method increasing processing time, and also interprets data for central storage, which has the implication that if the original is not available in future, new techniques to process original data will not be able to be applied to historical data. Roussev et al. (2013) examined the process of real-time digital forensics and triage by researching average times for different collection tasks under a triage scenario, within time constraints, with a focus on collecting the richest and most relevant information, which included; file system metadata, Windows registry, file metadata, and file content. They outlined a method of collecting relevant data by utilising Latency-optimized target acquisition (LOTA) whereby the data is collected sequentially, negating the need for a drive to continually seek to locate data.

Jones et al. (2012) outlined the implementation of a method of reducing the volume of material examined in CEM cases within the New South Wales Police State Electronic Evidence Branch by automated scripted sampling of digital forensic images to produce a smaller subset of data, which is reflective of the contents of the entire media. This method has merit, but is limited to investigations relating to CEM possession, whereas in other child related investigations full analysis is still required. Also, the process may be difficult to apply in various jurisdictions due to differing legislation, and does not address victim identification as a random sample of files is taken. In addition, there is no method of collection of common files which would be useful in providing intelligence in relation to the user, or overall trends across cases, although collection of important files can be easily added to the SEEB process (such as the process outlined in Chap. 4).

Shaw and Browne (2013) outlined a process of scanning physical media and interpreting data and presenting this to a practitioner, but this would not necessarily store the original data source files in a forensic container. With these methods, the original data is interpreted; there may be instances where new techniques are not able to be applied to the original data.

Raghavan (2013) discussed a solution to the volume problem is to use data reduction techniques and remove known and irrelevant data prior to analysis (However, it could be argued it would be better to remove irrelevant data prior to imaging). XIRAF uses a process of eliminating 'uninteresting' information subsequent to imaging and pre-processing (Bhoedjang et al. 2012). The focus of an applicable data reduction methodology could be to collect identified data which will provide the greatest information return, rather than collecting everything and then discarding known data. By first collecting only important data, the time savings in relation to collection and analysis can be vastly reduced, and the storage requirements are potentially vastly less than storing full images.

Breitinger and Roussev (2014) outlined a process of using *bytewise similar* hashing rather than *bytewise identical* hashing, to exclude known data and files, and introduced an automated method to evaluate matching results, but they did not outline processing timeframes, nor whether this is undertaken on full forensic images or data subsets. Breitinger et al. (2014) stated the time to compare known hash values using current processes was time consuming and that improved processes could achieve the same result in much faster timeframes, highlighting the results of experiments across 4,457 files comprising 1.9 GB of data in the order of seconds rather than minutes. Extrapolating this to current hard drives (with data volumes in the terabytes) results in lengthy timeframes for this process.

Brady et al. (2015) outlined a classification method with an aim to select potentially relevant data prior to processing, and stated that no effective solution had been found to identify potential artefacts on devices. Their proposed Digital Evidence Semantic Ontology (DESO) process focused on artefacts and relationships between them, but required further research and development to demonstrate applicability.

Greiner (2009) reminded us that there needs to be a focus on the goal of an investigation, knowing what needs to be answered, what is needed to answer it, how to get the data, and what the data tells us and, importantly, the principle of Occam's Razor, where the 'simplest answer is usually the right one, reminding us not to speculate, but let the data speak for itself.' The benefit of quickly analysing subset of data is that if the first round of collection does locate evidence, the practitioner can finalise the case and move on to the next one. If the first round of collection does not locate data of interest, then a forensic practitioner can return to the original media and conduct further analysis.

As digital forensic data consists of large volumes of structured and unstructured data, selecting the data which contains evidence or intelligence can be a challenge. Utilising statistical or random data reduction methods will likely result in missing crucial evidence (Beebe 2009; Shannon 2004). Data reduction methods applied to remote sensing images (Ma et al. 2014; Wang et al. 2014, 2015) are not necessarily applicable as these relate to streaming video data rather than the variety of structured and unstructured data commonly observed in forensic datasets, which can range from databases, compressed files, documents, pictures, text files, and also quite often commonly located commercial video files of television shows and movies rather than streamed video footage from satellites. When considering digital forensic data, such as: computer hard drives, portable storage, mobile phones, and network traffic, there are different requirements when compared with other general fields to which data mining is applied, such as: astrophysics, business and finance, and geospatial data.

A data reduction process of "feature selection" is potentially the most appropriate reduction method, whereby a subset of information is selected from an initial dataset (Kantardzic 2011). Stüttgen (2011) described a method of selective forensic imaging which required an investigator to select the files and data for imaging prior to collection. However, having a person review files and data for relevant information is time consuming; therefore there is a need for an automated process which rapidly collects data with a focus on that which will contribute to an investigation, including data of potential evidential and intelligence value.

2.5.3   Triage

Digital forensic triage is 'a process of sorting enquiries into groups based on the need for or likely benefit from examination' (Parsonage 2009). It was seen as a way to make better use of limited resources (Pollitt 2013). Digital triage has potential to assist with the data volume issue by identifying which items potentially contain evidence. In the context of this research, the focus is on triage processes applied to identify which item/s from a group are likely to contain evidence, such as a rapid examination by an experienced practitioner to determine which item may contain evidence. The focus is the technical triage process, rather than an Administrative Triage which is applied when determining case acceptance or case prioritisation.

Rogers et al. (2006) outlined a triage process model developed in the field on actual cases, court decisions, and prosecutor directions, designed to rapidly locate evidence and identify persons at risk by focussing on user profiles, timelines, internet activity, and case specific information, defining triage as 'a process in which things are ranked in terms of importance or priority.' LaVelle and Konrad

(2007) outlined a method for using the Microsoft Windows Robocopy command line tool via a GUI to preserve a subset of data, mainly aimed at large computer servers and storage systems. Casey (2009) highlighted the specialised expertise required when undertaking on-site examinations in a corporate or enterprise environment.

Reyes et al. (2007) introduced 'fast forensics' which referred to a process undertaken within the first few hours to locate information to use during an interview with a suspect. This usually related to on-site or field examination to locate evidence and intelligence to assist investigators to use in interview or other searches, but can also be applied in lab situations. Casey et al. (2009) discussed a triage process at a variety of levels, from the administrative decisions about thresholds to accepting cases, to a process of triage consisting of; survey/triage→preliminary examination→ in-depth examination, whereby cases are assessed and when accepted, decisions made to progress through the levels of examination based on each case and individual requirements. Garfinkel (2010) discussed a method of prioritization of analysis, in which a triage process is implemented to enable the practitioner to be presented with important information rapidly, and mentions a commercial system that can process media and display contents on a hand-held touch-screen user interface (IDEAL STRIKE) but this system is not widely marketed.

Roussev and Quates (2012) proposed a content triage process undertaken on forensic images, subsequent to the process of acquiring images of media. Using similarity digests and correlation hashing methodologies, with the aim of building a picture of the contents of forensic images, they applied the process to the M57 case study (Garfinkel et al. 2009a) to demonstrate the application of the proposed method across a range of forensic images. The process of imaging larger and larger drives could place an undue burden on the time to undertake a rapid triage, and hence it would be beneficial to first undertake a data reduction process to rapidly improve the triage timeframe (as per the process outlined in Chap. 4).

Overill et al. (2013) outlined a process for managing triage within a digital forensic lab with investigations involving multiple devices, based on the underlying crime type of an investigation and the role of the digital evidence, i.e. whether it was central (specific), or auxiliary to an investigation. The process utilised automated triage software tools, and the triage process would reportedly stop when a value criteria for a specific investigation type was reached.

Shaw and Browne (2013) focused on *technical triage* rather than *administrative triage*, and highlighted the risk of inadequately trained personnel reviewing artefacts which require a high degree of knowledge and experience in digital forensic analysis to interpret. The technical triage process they outlined involved booting a suspect device with a Linux OS and then conducting a thorough scan of the entire media, parsing file systems and recovering artefacts from unallocated space, interpreting data, and storing the results in report format. Marturana and Tacconi (2013) proposed an automated method which gathered file and data statistical information, which could be applied during *live* or *post-mortem* situations, and provided an examiner information summarising the file types contained on media, such as a hard drive or mobile device.

O'Connor (2004) discussed the use of PXE boot in a corporate environment involving a large number of systems in an endeavour to review systems and identify those potentially containing evidence. Koopmans and James (2013) discussed an automatic triage process using PXE boot as applied to networked computers to locate specific hosts which contain information matching key terms setup from a central server, and highlighted specific investigations where the process had been successfully utilised.

Vidas et al. (2014) outlined the use of OpenLV (previously LiveView) and its application as a triage tool, and whilst this tool enabled a forensic image or physical device to be booted in a virtual environment without changing the original data, it did not perform any analysis, relying on an examiner to traverse a computer as a user would, potentially missing data which is not usually presented easily to a user, such as Registry data, or information held in other databases (Internet History, Chat History, Deleted Emails, etc.). Shiaeles et al. (2013) compared three triage tools (TriageIR, TR3Secure, and Kludge) and reported on their suitability, concluding that not one tool is able to fulfil the needs of every situation.

Dalins et al. (2015) outlined a triage method useful to identify known materials of interest, such as illicit images, in minimal time by using a Monte-Carlo File System search. This system was applicable for use to determine illicit images in a timely manner, although this was not as applicable to general investigations, and was quite specific for illicit image investigations where evidence must be located at the time of identification.

Hitchcock et al. (2016) proposed a tiered methodology for digital field triage by non-specialists. The Digital Field Triage Model consisted of four phases designed for use by a digital field triage member rather than a specialist. Digital Field Triage (DFT) members were trained in computer triage using a custom built Ubuntu based tool and mobile device triage using a commercial solution. The process has been implemented in the Royal Canadian Mounted Police (RCMP) Canada, and resulted in 1,878 DFT examinations.

Koven et al. (2016) presented "Intelligent Visual Email Search and Triage" (InVEST), a methodology to search and discover evidence and information in large email datasets using a visual analytic approach.

A triage process has potential to quickly identify which evidence items are likely to contain evidential data and, hence, once the identified data is examined and reported, there may be an opportunity to close the investigation and move on to the next one. Software is available to conduct initial triage of digital media, such as ADF Triage, EnCase Portable, and AccessData Triage. Many of these tools interpret the data and present the findings in a report, without opportunity to collect the original files for archival storage, or collect data in proprietary format which doesn't provide for subsequent processing, data mining, or analysis with alternative tools. There is an opportunity to undertake research to address the triage process with a method of collecting and reviewing a subset of data quickly, which serves the purpose of a triage to quickly identify media with evidential data, and also serve to support other forensic analysis purposes; data mining, intelligence analysis, knowledge discovery, archival, and retrieval.

A data reduction process which is undertaken prior to the use of FFE, or other tools, can alleviate the concern of scanning and only retaining interpreted information. Collecting the original source files can enable future processing of the original source data with a potential to uncover additional information as newly discovered information extraction methods are discovered. An ability to apply a variety of tools to a data subset to uncover additional information, and an ability to store digital forensic data subsets to enable cross case and cross device analysis with smaller storage requirements is another objective of a reduction process. By collecting the original files in a logical forensic container, additional processes can be applied to the data to potentially gain a better understanding of the information, rather than an interpretation at a specific point in time.

2.6 Other Proposed Solutions to the Data Volume Challenge

There have been other proposed solutions to the issue of increasing volume of data seized for analysis, including distributed and parallel processing, visualisation, digital forensic as a service (DFaaS), and the use of artificial intelligence techniques.

Parallel and distributed processing offers a potential to speed up analysis of forensic data. Roussev and Richard (2004) examined the application of distributed processing in an effort to deal with the exponential growth in data presented for analysis, and outlined a method for dividing the tasks of indexing and searching across multiple workstations to undertake these tasks in a timely manner. Lee et al. (2008) outlined the application of a Tarari content processor[1] in relation to searching of data, concluding that there were positive benefits, but that further research is necessary. Nance et al. (2009) stated that whilst there have been some developments in relation to implementing parallel processing of forensic data (Access Data Distributed Network Attack for password recovery), there are other areas which could benefit from parallel processing, such as data carving and generating timeline reports. They also mentioned that the process of imaging could benefit from parallel processing. However, the process of imaging relies on the speed of the source media, and attempting to have multiple processes calling for access to different sections of a hard drive could confuse the hardware controller and potentially lead to longer read/seek times, rather than speeding up the process.

---

[1]Tarari content processors are designed to distribute processing of data across multiple threads to speed up regular expression search times, and other functions, and are often used in intrusion detection applications (LSI 2011).

Ayers (2009) defined a series of requirements for second generation forensic tools, including parallel processing, data storage, and accuracy. Pringle and Sutherland (2008) examined the process of developing a high capacity forensic computer system using grid computing systems. Pringle and Burgess (2014) discussed previous research and highlighted the inherent issues with current distributed tools, for example the use of central storage, and proposed a cluster based file storage system (ClusterFS) and methodology in an endeavour to balance and distribute processing, with research and further testing underway. Garfinkel (2012a) stated that efforts to utilise multi-threading and high performance computing have been problematic, although some successful results have been achieved. Parallel processing has potential to assist with processing increasing volumes of data, but may not scale as rapidly as the rate of data growth.

Marziale et al. (2007) discussed the use of Graphic Processing Units (GPU) in experiments to evaluate offloading processing to a GPU in comparison with a multicore Central Processing Unit (CPU). They concluded that the use of GPUs can provide positive benefits to processing times, especially in relation to binary string searches, and that future research is worthwhile. To date major commercial forensic software companies have changed the underlying methods of storing and processing information, and have introduced some parallel and distributed processing options for their forensic analysis software (AccessDataCorporation 2010; DFI_News 2011). As the size of digital forensic investigations continues to increase, current tools still take considerable time to process the increasing volume of data (Marziale et al. 2007). Hence multiple strategies may be required to address the current data volume challenges, without relying on one single potential solution.

Beebe (2009) discussed 'intelligent analytical approaches' and the use of analytical algorithms to reduce the time it takes to locate information, allowing investigators to get to relevant data quickly and reduce the superfluous information in a typical case. Sheldon (2005b) discussed concepts for the future of digital forensics, stating that the pace of development in technology affects digital forensics, and that in an ideal world, future digital forensic systems will be able to utilise artificial intelligence to assimilate the contents of digital media, and use inference rules to produce information that can guide an analyst when conducting analysis (at that time, hoped to be possible by 2015). Rules can be established to interpret differing data structures, combined with an ability to learn from each case it is used on, and linkage to a global network of information, to assist examiners (Sheldon 2005b). Hoelz et al. (2009) outlined the potential application of artificial intelligence techniques to digital forensic data through a multi agent system and case-based reasoning to analyse and correlate data, and presented the results to an examiner, and included the application of a distributed platform in the experiments.

Marturana et al. (2015) discussed a machine learning approach to multimedia forensics and digital forensic triage, and highlighted the increasing large volume of multimedia data. Using Waikato Environment for Knowledge Analysis (WEKA) they used a test data corpus to classify the data holdings from real-world data to determine which devices contained relevant versus non-relevant data. This process has application with multimedia examinations, but is not applicable to general investigations.

Alink et al. (2006) developed an approach to the volume of data problem which consists of the following; feature extraction and analysis, XML based output from various tools, and XML database storage and query. They developed a prototype system called XIRAF (XML Information Retrieval Approach to digital forensics) which extracted information from forensic images and stored the information in a database, accessed via a web interface. They outlined times to process data, including; hashing files can take several hours, extracting EXIF data takes several hours, and parsing unallocated space also takes several hours. Bearing in mind these tasks are undertaken consecutively, this added up to considerable time to process data, at that time stated to be tested on forensic images ranging from 40 to 240 GB. With today's hard drive sizes in the many terabytes, the processing times would be considerably larger if new techniques are not implemented.

Bhoedjang et al. (2012) updated the progress of developing XIRAF (six years later) to consume larger data volumes. Search functionality had been implemented, using indexed search methods. Remote access was now available using a web interface, allowing a wider range of clients to access forensic data, including experts and non-experts; analysts, lawyers, and detectives. User management was addressed with the web interface, which also included project management. The XIRAF system automated many tasks, freeing up specialists for higher level tasks, and by presenting information in a common format, removed the need for an examiner to understand the technical details of different forensic software, although they stated the amount of data was still potentially overwhelming. Pre-processing utilised commodity hardware, and was reported to take a day to run a single pass over input data, even with previous tools being merged, and the implementation of tools being run in parallel. However, processing times are stated to be acceptable, and although distributed processing of single images was thought to significantly complicate the system, it was stated to be not clear if this would justify the cost of implementation (Bhoedjang et al. 2012).

van Baar et al. (2014) further discussed the application of XIRAF as a whole of process model, applied in the Netherlands, with implementation as Digital Forensics as a Service (DFaaS). They highlighted that traditional forensic labs generally make specialists responsible for a variety of administrative tasks, and hence have less time to perform specialised analysis. In the DFaaS implementation they had a team of support personnel, responsible for administration of; applications, databases, storage, infrastructure, and other systems. This freed up specialists to perform specialised tasks. In relation to DFaaS being applied in a real world situation, they stated that it would be beneficial for digital information to be available within the first few days to investigators, but in traditional systems, this is not the case.

van Beek et al. (2015) further updated the experience with Digital Forensics as a Service Xiraf and the development of Hanksen in an effort to provide timely processing for analysis of a wide variety of devices and data, collaboration between digital investigators and detectives, encompassing design principles, security, privacy, logging, and transparency.

Teelink and Erbacher (2006) outlined the application of non-hierarchical and hierarchical visualisation techniques to folder tree structures of hard disk drives, and conducted experiments comparing visualisation with text searches, concluding that visualisation methods have potential benefits to forensic analysis. Furthermore in relation to visualisation, Olsson and Boldt (2009) discussed timestamp information and how this is a common denominator for the large variety of structured and unstructured data common to digital forensic holdings, and could be used to create visualisations of digital forensic data. Alink et al. (2006) used the timestamp information from multiple forensic tools to produce timeline visualisations which includes data from multiple tools and evidence in the XIRAF prototype. Stevens (2004) examined time information in relation to correlation from different sources, synchronisation, and a model to simulate clock behaviour to address errors to enable the unification of clock information into single time lines.

Gupta et al. (2016) applied mathematical optimization approaches to selected resources for digital forensic investigations with multiple investigators. This was undertaken by allocating investigators with the maximum available time within a set of investigators. However, in experience, there are often few investigators to select from, and usually one investigator has responsibility to carry out the review of digital media. Hence there is usually only one person available or with the requisite and appropriate knowledge to undertake a review and having to explain all facets of an investigation to another reviewer would add time to the process. The algorithm proposed does not take into account the knowledge of an investigator, nor the does it factor in the time to bring another person up to speed in relation to an investigation. The forensic expertise of an investigator is discussed, but this is more in relation to their expertise, and not case-specific knowledge, which is a large aspect of a timely review.

Khan et al. (2007) outlined a proposed method of generating timeline activity from digital evidence by applying post-event reconstruction using neural network techniques. Raghavan (2013) discussed the challenges of generated a unified timeline across multiple sources of evidence, which include time zone interpretation, clock skew, and syntax. Schatz and Clark (2006) discussed time and date issues in relation to forensic analysis, studying clock skew and corroboration.

Buchholz and Tjaden (2007) undertook a study in relation to the clocks of hosts connected to the Internet within the scope of forensic investigations. Marrington et al. (2011) produced prototype software which detects inconsistencies in computer activity timelines. As time and date issues can be crucial in a forensic examination, confirming the accuracy of data and the subsequent forming of subsequent conclusions is necessary to ensure accuracy, and acceptance of evidence in court (Boyd 2004). Visualisation techniques are an important aspect to be considered, along with a comprehensive approach, without relying on one method or technique to address the volume challenge.

Beebe (2009) observed that forensic research has followed the digital forensic process, in that the initial focus of research has been on response and collection (hence hardware write blockers and live response procedures being developed), and the focus of research was now swinging towards analysis and presentation (Beebe 2009).

In the United States Department of Justice (2016) Audit report, the Director of the New Jersey RCFL stated the solution to reduce the backlog of cases is to bring in additional examiners, and estimated that it takes between 14 and 24 months for a new employee to be trained as a certified examiner. It was also reported that the NJRCFL tried three alternative methods to reduce the backlog; Digital Crime Analysis Position (DCAP), Virtual Machine Forensics Platform (VMFP), and Centralized Imaging (CI). DCAP provided for remote review of cases, but 'while this was supposed to alleviate some of the backlog issues, it may have actually caused some additional delays' (Justice 2016). VMFP enables examiners to access multiple cases at once, and CI is a tool to image numerous computers simultane- ously. 'According to the NJRCFL Director, Centralized Imaging has worked for the NJRCFL, especially with exigent, large cases; however, it also has not helped reduce the backlog as much as he thought it would' and 'according to the NJRCFL Director, RCFL examiners have found that the Virtual Machine Forensic Platform was more troublesome than helpful in streamlining the examination process.' (Justice 2016) Hence the three methods as tried were not able to address the backlog issue.

2.7   Discussion

As outlined, there has been much discussion regarding the data volume challenge, and calls for research into the application of data mining and other techniques to address the problem. Nevertheless, there has been very little published work in relation to a method or framework to apply data mining techniques, or other methods to reduce or analyse the large volume of real-world data. In addition, the value of extracting or using intelligence from digital forensic data has had minimal discussion.

There are a variety of research fields which have potential to impact the volume data challenge, including Knowledge Discovery, Knowledge Management, Data Mining, and Criminal Intelligence Analysis. Knowledge Discovery and Management are overall processes to extract valuable knowledge from data (Cios and Kurgan 2005). Data mining is a step of the knowledge discovery process and may offer a way to comprehend the large volume of seized data (Fayyad et al. 1996b). Whilst there have been many calls for research in relation to the large volume issue, which include whether data mining methodologies can be applied to digital forensic data (Beebe and Clark 2005; Palmer 2001), there is very little published which progresses this. This is, perhaps, because digital forensic research is relatively new compared to other forensic science disciplines or the information security discipline. For example, *Digital Investigation*, the only journal dedicated to Digital Forensics with an impact factor, which ranks six (and is the top digital forensic publication) in Google Scholar's (general) Forensic Science category,[2] is only in its 11th year in 2014.

Significant gaps remain in relation to applying data mining methodology to digital forensic data, including a methodology which can be applied to real world data, the benefits which may be observed, and the most appropriate methodology to achieve the desired results including; a reduction in analysis time, a method of archiving and retrieving data, a rapid triage process, and a methodology to gain knowledge from seized data. Whilst data mining alone may not be an overall solution to the many issues raised, it will perhaps have best application in relation to intelligence and understanding of disparate case information to provide an overall increase in knowledge, and perhaps should be researched with that in mind.

It was observed that there is minimal published information relating to the average processing times of average evidence amounts per year, such as applying common forensic analysis tasks to common data. There is an opportunity to use a standard corpus of data and apply common processing techniques to this, and record the timeframe for processing, extrapolating this to hard drive sizes of the time. This would serve to highlight whether there is a growing gap in processing times, and when undertaken for a period of time, serve to show whether processing techniques are improving analysis timeframes.

There is great potential to develop a data reduction methodology which serves to collect a subset of important information for the purposes of triage, rapid analysis, data mining, intelligence analysis, and archiving. Data reduction techniques have perhaps the greatest opportunity to influence the various stages of forensic analysis, and also to provide benefits to other areas not generally discussed (i.e. intelligence, archiving, and knowledge of trends).

Another major gap relates to the use of intelligence gained during forensic analysis, which has potentially a large benefit to policing agencies, and yet remains unaddressed. The current focus is on attending to urgent jobs, with no time to consider other matters which may provide valuable input to current investigations. Historically, there has very little discussion of a methodology to utilise the intelligence gained from one investigation to assist with other investigations, nor to build a body of knowledge inherent in historical cases. In addition, the use of open and closed source intelligence for investigations could provide a manner of improving the time and value of analysis of digital forensic investigations. For example, information stored on a phone seized for one investigation may provide information to other seemingly unrelated investigations. Without an intelligence or knowledge management process, this information or linkage remains undiscovered. Using knowledge management, intelligence analysis, and data mining methodology, it is envisioned that a large volume of information could be aggregated into common data holdings, and include the capability for rapid searches to link associated information and assist in investigations.

---

[2]http://scholar.google.com.au/citations?view_op=top_venues&hl=en&vq=soc_forensicscience; last accessed 26 May 2014.

Whilst many of the problems posed by the increasing volume of data are addressed in part by new developments in technology, another challenge is that the law is somewhat slower to address issues relating to digital forensic analysis (McKemmish 1999). Hence, any new methodologies must abide to the legal environment to which they are being applied, as the pace of change in law makes it difficult to implement unique solutions to challenges. Dr Eugene Spafford (as cited in Palmer 2001) stated that a comprehensive approach to academic research is required to address the range of challenges, not just the technical ones, and include social, legal, and procedural. Procedural guidelines and practices which focus on collecting every piece of data in an investigation can lead to a requirement to thoroughly examine large volumes of data. Social issues relate to the storage of data for long periods of time, which use resources that could be used to address other issues as opposed to storage concerns. Legal issues relate to the ability of law to keep pace with the changes in technology.

There is an opportunity to develop a framework for digital forensic practitioners to apply data mining and intelligence analysis techniques to digital forensic data to reduce the time to collect and gain an understanding of the data seized. Future research opportunities exist in relation to determining appropriate data reduction and data mining techniques to apply to the volume of structured and unstructured data atypical of seized evidential data. There is a need for digital forensic data mining and intelligence analysis techniques to be developed and tested against test data and real world (anonymised) data to determine an appropriate methodology or methodologies which can be applied in real world situations in an effort to address the digital forensic volume data issue.

There is much discussion about growing backlogs of cases awaiting analysis, yet few real-world figures are available to enable accurate understanding of the problem. It would be appropriate for actual figures to be available, although it is understood that many (if not all) agencies would not allow this information to be released for public discussion. The information in the FBI RCFL Annual Reports is of great value to enable an understanding of the growing size of data and number of cases each year over a period of time. Further information relating to device volume, number of devices, timeframes, backlogs, number of cases with data in cloud storage, imaging times, processing times, analysis times, review times, report volumes, and successful presentations in a legal context, would all be relevant to enable academics and researchers to understand where to focus their work.

In addition, the process of triage has been widely discussed, including special journals and publications devoted to the topic, and many methods have been proposed. A gap in relation to research into the real world application of these methodologies, with supportive figures would serve to highlight the impact of triage methods, and which are successful and applicable to an organisation.

Whilst many concepts are put forward to improve triage, imaging, processing, and analysis, there is little discussion about scaling these to the volume of current case requirements. Some methods are applied to very small data volumes, and when extrapolated to current case sizes would result in many hours or days of processing required. It would be appropriate to scale these methods to apply to real-world data volumes, and also make better use of real-world data or a corpus reflective of that (such as that of Garfinkel 2012a). It would also be beneficial to undertake common imaging and processing tasks using a range of common forensic tools across a common forensic corpus to compare processing times over a period of years, to determine if there have been improvements in technology and tools.

There are also research gaps in relation to the effectiveness of the various approaches in relation to which are applicable in practicable terms. Future research could examine the effectiveness of the various proposed solutions in terms of evidence identification in a large corpus, and in terms of the admissibility of the data into court. For example, a review of the acceptance of triaged evidence or evidence derived from data reduction in a legal environment, and include a review of any concerns raised in relation to whether a data reduction process is potentially missing exculpatory evidence.

The legal issues raised by Spafford (as cited in Palmer 2001) related to ensuring a compliance with law and legal procedures, as there is little point in undertaking research and deploying advanced technology if it doesn't comply with the law and rules in the environment which it is deployed. RFC 3227 lists the legal consider-ations in relation to computer evidence, including the need to ensure it is; Admissible, Authentic, Complete, Reliable, and Believable (Brezinski and Killalea 2002). Where 'Complete' is listed, it is in relation to telling 'the whole story, and not just a particular perspective', and does not necessitate a need to image every-thing. As long as legal issues are considered when determining new methods to copy, store, and process data, it will be far easier to gain acceptance from forensic practitioners within a legal environment. Future efforts of research should also abide with legal, social, and procedural guidelines, such that legal considerations are compliant, timeliness of processes ensures social acceptance, and procedural issues in relation to adoption of techniques are discussed.

2.8 Summary

The literature survey identified that research gaps exist in relation to the digital forensic data volume challenge. For example, there remains a need for appropriate data reduction techniques, data mining, intelligence analysis, and the use of open and closed source information. This should include research into the application of processes in a real world environment, and its acceptance in Courts and other tribunals.

Data mining offers a potential solution to understanding the increasing volume of data, but may be more suited as an intelligence and knowledge tool, rather than an evidence focussed tool. Understanding the intelligence value of digital forensic data is a gap, and making use of this knowledge from the volume of data is an untapped resource which agencies should consider. Merging disparate data into a common body of knowledge may provide linkages which are currently unknown. A survey of current processing and analysis tools using a standard corpus would serve to provide an understanding of the current time for these tasks, and ongoing comparisons would serve to measure the progress of forensic tools.

Triage processes are well discussed, and perhaps seen as a solution to the growing volume of devices and data. Further research would be appropriate to assess the influence of various triage processes on real world devices and data to determine the most applicable methodology to deploy, which also provides for future needs, and a review of the acceptance of triaged evidence in a legal environment, including whether the process is potentially missing exculpatory evidence. A review of backlog of cases within agencies is also needed to quantify the actual extent of the problem, as this information is often anecdotal, confidentiality issues notwithstanding.

A data reduction process holds potential to influence a range of digital forensic stages; such as collection, processing and analysis, and provide for intelligence, knowledge, and future needs. Any methodology developed should follow a comprehensive framework to address; data reduction, review, analysis, data mining, intelligence analysis, data storage, archiving, and retrieval.

As highlighted in the literature review, there remains a need for research and an applicable method to reduce the volume of digital forensic data for analysis for evidence and intelligence. Technology is rapidly increasing, and is increasingly used by consumers, business, and government to store vast amounts of data.

Devices and data are increasingly used by criminals, and are a target of criminals. Security of devices are, in the main, adequately addressed, however digital forensic investigations are under increasing pressure to do more with less in the current economic environment.

Law enforcement agencies and investigators have a need to access an increasing volume of data and devices. Difficulties arise when attempting to apply traditional computer forensic methods of investigation to a growing volume of disparate data and devices. In addition, the initial identification of the existence of evidential data can be difficult, due to the volume and number of data and devices. Hence, there is a need for a forensically sound process to rapidly collect and review data from a range of devices, and provide a mechanism for a practitioner to review the data in a timely manner to locate relevant evidence and intelligence.

In undertaking secondary research in relation to published material, it was apparent there is minimal information available to guide investigators in relation to data reduction and rapid analysis methodologies. This highlights a need for research to be undertaken in relation to the data volume and identification points for an examiner to quickly look for evidence and intelligence. This process needs to be applicable for a range of computers and mobile devices, highlighting a need to research methods of analysis for computers and mobile devices. This is further explored in Volume 2: Quick Analysis for Evidence and Intelligence.

The data reduction and analysis process must abide by the principals of digital forensic analysis, and guidelines and rules of evidence as communicated by Courts and legal bodies. If any proposed process is not undertaken in a forensically sound manner, the entire investigation in relation to the data may be put at risk, and the evidence not accepted in court or legal proceedings.

In the following chapter, the digital forensic data reduction framework and processes are detailed.

References

Abraham, T. (2006). Event sequence mining to develop profiles for computer forensic investigation purposes. In *ACSW Frontiers'06: Proceedings of the 2006 Australasian workshops on Grid computing and e-Research* (pp. 145–153).

AccessDataCorporation. (2010). *Divide & Conquer: Overcoming computer forensic backlog through distributed processing and division of labor* White Paper.

ACPO. (2006). *Good practice guidelines for computer based evidence v4.0*, Association of Chief Police Officers. Retrieved March 5, 2014, www.7safe.com/electronic_evidence.

Adelstein, F. (2006). Live forensics: diagnosing your system without killing it first. *Communications of the ACM, 49*(2), 63–66.

Al Fahdi, M., Clarke, N., Li, F., & Furnell, S. (2016). A suspect-oriented intelligent and automated computer forensic analysis. *Digital Investigation, 18,* 65–76.

Alink, W., Bhoedjang, R. A. F., Boncz, P. A., & de Vries, A. P. (2006). XIRAF—XML-based indexing and querying for digital forensics, *Digital Investigation, 3,* 50–58.

Alzaabi, M., Jones, A., & Martin, T. A. (2013). An ontology-based forensic analysis tool. *Journal of Digital Forensics, Security & Law, 2013,* 121–135. (Conference Supplement).

Ayers, D. (2009). A second generation computer forensic analysis system. *Digital Investigation, 6,* S34–S42.

Baggili, I., & Breitinger, F. (2015). Data sources for advancing cyber forensics: what the social world has to offer. In *2015 AAAI Spring Symposium Series.*

Beebe, N. (2009). Digital forensic research: the good, the bad and the unaddressed. In Advances in Digital Forensics (pp. 17–36). Springer.

Beebe, N., & Clark, J. (2005). Dealing with terabyte data sets in digital investigations. In *Advances in Digital Forensics* (pp. 3–16).

Bell, L. (2013). *Seagate launches 4 TB hard disk engineered for video content*, The Inquirer, Retrieved June 22, from http://www.theinquirer.net/inquirer/news/2269518/seagate-launches-4tb-hard-disk-engineered-for-video-content.

Bhoedjang, R. A. F., van Ballegooij, A. R., van Beek, H. M. A., van Schie, J. C., Dillema, F. W., van Baar, R. B., et al. (2012). Engineering an online computer forensic service. *Digital Investigation, 9*(2), 96–108.

Biggs, S., & Vidalis, S. (2009). Cloud computing: the impact on digital forensic investigations. In *IEEE International Conference for Internet Technology and Secured Transactions (ICITST 2009)* (pp. 1–6). IEEE.

Boyd, C. (2004). Time and date issues in forensic computing-a case study. *Digital Investigation, 1* (1), 18–23.

Brady, O., Overill, R., & Keppens, J. (2015). DESO: addressing volume and variety in large-scale criminal cases. *Digital Investigation, 15,* 72–82.

Breitinger, F., & Roussev, V. (2014). Automated evaluation of approximate matching algorithms on real data. *Digital Investigation, 11*(Suppl. 1), S10–S17.

Breitinger, F., Baier, H., & White, D. (2014). On the database lookup problem of approximate matching. *Digital Investigation, 11*(Suppl. 1), S1–S9.

Brezinski, D., & Killalea, T. (2002). RFC 3227–Guidelines for evidence collection and archiving.

Brown, R., Pham, B., & de Vel, O. (2005). Design of a digital forensics image mining system. In *Knowledge-Based Intelligent Information and Engineering Systems* (pp. 395–404).

Buchholz, F., & Tjaden, B. (2007). A brief study of time. *Digital Investigation, 4,* 31–42.

Carvey, H. (2011). *Windows Registry Forensics: Advanced Digital Forensic Analysis of the Windows Registry.* Elsevier.

Case, A., Cristina, A., Marziale, L., Richard, G.G., & Roussev, V. (2008). FACE: automated digital evidence discovery and correlation. *Digital Investigation, 5,* S65–S75.

Casey, E. (2009). "Dawn raids" bring a new form in incident response. *Digital Investigation, 5*(3–4), 73–74.

Casey, E. (2010). Digital dust: Evidence in every nook and cranny. *Digital Investigation, 6*(3–4), 93–94.

Casey, E. (2014). Growing societal impact of digital forensics and incident response. *Digital Investigation, 11*(1), 1–2.

Casey, E., Ferraro, M., & Nguyen, L. (2009). Investigation delayed is justice denied: proposals for expediting forensic examinations of digital evidence. *Journal of Forensic Sciences, 54*(6), 1353–1364.

Casey, E., Katz, G., & Lewthwaite, J. (2013). Honing digital forensic processes. *Digital Investigation, 10*(2), 138–147.

Cios, K., & Kurgan, L. (2005). Trends in data mining and knowledge discovery. In *Advanced Techniques in Knowledge Discovery and Data Mining* (pp. 1–26).

Coughlin, T. (2001). High density hard disk drive trends in the USA. *Journal Magnetics Society of Japan, 25*(3/1), 111–120.

Craiger, J., Pollitt, M., & Swauger, J. (2005). Law enforcement and digital evidence. *Handbook of Information Security, 2,* 739–777.

Culley, A. (2003). Computer forensics: past, present and future. *Information Security Technical Report, 8*(2), 32–36.

Dalins, J., Wilson, C., & Carman, M. (2015). Monte-carlo filesystem search–A crawl strategy for digital forensics. *Digital Investigation, 13,* 58–71.

DFI_News. (2011). *Guidance Software Announces EnCase Forensic Version 7.* Retrieved January 26, from http://www.dfinews.com/product-releases/2011/06/guidance-software-announces-encase-forensic-version-7#.UuR2hLRe6Uk.

Fayyad, U., Piatetsky-Shapiro, G., & Smyth, P. (1996a). From data mining to knowledge discovery in databases. *AI magazine, 17*(3), 37.

Fayyad, U., Piatetsky-Shapiro, G., & Smyth, P. (1996b). The KDD process for extracting useful knowledge from volumes of data. *Communications of the ACM, 39*(11), 27–34.

Fayyad, U., Piatetsky-Shapiro, G., & Smyth, P. (1996c). Knowledge discovery and data mining: Towards a unifying framework. *Knowledge Discovery and Data Mining,* 82–88.

FBI_RCFL. (2003–2012). *FBI Regional Computer Forensic Laboratory Annual Reports 2003–2012,* FBI, Quantico.

Ferraro, M. M., & Russell, A. (2004). Current issues confronting well-established computer-assisted child exploitation and computer crime task forces. *Digital Investigation, 1*(1), 7–15.

Fowler, K. (2012). Hadoop Forensics, Tackling the elephant in the room. In *SecTor 2012: Security Education Conference Toronto October 1–3, 2012 MTCC Toronto.*

Garfinkel, S. (2006). Forensic feature extraction and cross-drive analysis. *Digital Investigation, 3,* 71–81.

Garfinkel, S., Farrell, P., Roussev, V., & Dinolt, G. (2009a). *Bringing science to digital forensics with standardized forensic corpora,* DFRWS 2009, Montreal, Canada. Retrieved September 9, from http://digitalcorpora.org/corpora/disk-images.

Garfinkel, S. (2010). Digital forensics research: The next 10 years. *Digital Investigation, 7,* S64–S73.

Garfinkel, S. (2012a). Lessons learned writing digital forensics tools and managing a 30 TB digital evidence corpus. *Digital Investigation, 9,* S80–S89.

Garfinkel, S. (2012b). Digital forensics XML and the DFXML toolset. *Digital Investigation, 8*(3–4), 161–174.

Garfinkel, S. (2013). Digital media triage with bulk data analysis and bulk_extractor. *Computers & Security, 32,* 56–72.

Garfinkel, S., Farrell, P., Roussev, V., & Dinolt, G. (2009b). Bringing science to digital forensics with standardized forensic corpora. *Digital Investigation, 6,* S2–S11.

Gartner. (2013). *IT Glossary: Big Data.* Retrieved July 21, from http://www.gartner.com/it-glossary/big-data/.

Gogolin, G. (2010). The digital crime tsunami. *Digital Investigation, 7*(1–2), 3–8.

Greiner, L. (2009). Sniper forensics. *netWorker, 13*(4), 8–10.

Grier, J., & Richard, G. G. (2015). Rapid forensic acquisition of large media with sifting collectors. *Digital Investigation, 14*(2015), S34–S44.

Growchowski, E. (1998). Emerging trends in data storage on magnetic hard disk drives. *Datatech (September 1998)* (pp. 11–16). ICG Publishing.

Gupta, J. N., Kalaimannan, E., & Yoo, S.-M. (2016). A heuristic for maximizing investigation effectiveness of digital forensic cases involving multiple investigators. *Computers & Operations Research, 69,* 1–9.

Halboob, W., Mahmod, R., Abulaish, M., Abbas, H., & Saleem, K. (2015). Data warehousing based computer forensics investigation framework. In *2015 12th International Conference on Information Technology-New Generations (ITNG).*

Hand, D.J., Mannila, H., & Smyth, P. (2001). *Principles of data mining.* MIT Press.

Hearst, M.A. (1999). Untangling text data mining. In *Proceedings of the 37th Annual Meeting of the Association for Computational Linguistics on Computational Linguistics* (pp. 3–10). Association for Computational Linguistics.

Hicks, C., Beebe, N., & Haliscak, B. (2016). Extending web mining to digital forensics text mining. In *Information Systems Security and Privacy (SIGSEC) AMCIS 2016.*

Hitchcock, B., Le-Khac, N.-A., & Scanlon, M. (2016). Tiered forensic methodology model for Digital Field Triage by non-digital evidence specialists. *Digital Investigation, 16,* S75–S85.

Hoelz, B., Ralha, C., & Geeverghese, R. (2009). Artificial intelligence applied to computer forensics. In *SAC'09: Proceedings of the 2009 ACM symposium on Applied Computing* (pp. 883–888). ACM.

Huang, J., Yasinsac, A., & Hayes, P. J. (2010). Knowledge sharing and reuse in digital forensics. In *2010 Fifth IEEE International Workshop on Systematic Approaches to Digital Forensic Engineering (SADFE)* (pp. 73–78). IEEE.

INTERPOL. (2004). In *Proceedings of the 14th INTERPOL Forensic Science Symposium.*

Iqbal, F., Hadjidj, R., Fung, B. C. M., & Debbabi, M. (2008). A novel approach of mining write-prints for authorship attribution in e-mail forensics. *Digital Investigation, 5,* S42–S51.

Iqbal, F., Binsalleeh, H., Fung, B., & Debbabi, M. (2010). Mining writeprints from anonymous e-mails for forensic investigation. *Digital Investigation, 7*(1), 56–64.

Jones, B., Pleno, S., & Wilkinson, M. (2012). The use of random sampling in investigations involving child abuse material. *Digital Investigation, 9,* S99–S107.

Justice, UDo. (2015). *Office of the inspector general. Audit of the Federal Bureau of Investigation's Philadelphia Regional Computer Forensic Laboratory,* https://oig.justice.gov/reports/2015/a1514.pdf.

Justice, UDo. (2016). *Office of the inspector general. Audit of the Federal Bureau of Investigation's New Jersey Regional Computer Forensic Laboratory,* https://oig.justice.gov/reports/2016/a1611.pdf.

Kantardzic, M. (2011). *Data mining: concepts, models, methods, and algorithms.* John Wiley & Sons.

Kenneally, E., & Brown, C. (2005). Risk sensitive digital evidence collection. *Digital Investigation, 2*(2), 101–119.

Khan, M., Chatwin, C., & Young, R. (2007). A framework for post-event timeline reconstruction using neural networks. *Digital Investigation, 4*(3–4), 146–157.

Kohavi, R., Rothleder, N., & Simoudis, E. (2002). Emerging trends in business analytics. *Communications of the ACM, 45*(8), 45–48.

Koopmans, M. B., & James, J. I. (2013). Automated network triage. *Digital Investigation, 10*(2), 129–137.

Koven, J., Bertini, E., Dubois, L., & Memon, N. (2016). InVEST: intelligent visual email search and triage. *Digital Investigation, 18,* S138–S148.

LaVelle, C., & Konrad, A. (2007). FriendlyRoboCopy: a GUI to RoboCopy for computer forensic investigators. *Digital Investigation, 4*(1), 16–23.

Lee, W., & Stolfo, S. J. (2000). *Data mining approaches for intrusion detection*, Defense Technical Information Center.

Lee, J., Un, S., & Hong, D. (2008). High-speed search using Tarari content processor in digital forensics. *Digital Investigation, 5,* S91–S95.

Leimich, P., Harrison, J., & Buchanan, W. J. (2016). A RAM triage methodology for Hadoop HDFS forensics. *Digital Investigation.*

Lillis, D., Becker, B., O'Sullivan, T., & Scanlon, M. (2016). Current challenges and future research areas for digital forensic investigation. arXiv:1604.03850.

LSI. (2011). LSI Tarari Content Processor Family Enhanced with High-Performance, Low-Latency Solution, http://www.lsi.com/about/newsroom/Pages/20100426apr.aspx.

Ma, Y., Wang, L., Liu, P., & Ranjan, R. (2014). Towards building a data-intensive index for big data computing–a case study of remote sensing data processing. *Information Sciences.*

Marrington, A., Baggili, I., Mohay, G., & Clark, A. (2011). CAT Detect (Computer Activity Timeline Detection): a tool for detecting inconsistency in computer activity timelines. *Digital Investigation, 8,* S52–S61.

Marturana, F., & Tacconi, S. (2013). A Machine Learning-based Triage methodology for automated categorization of digital media. *Digital Investigation, 10*(2), 193–204.

Marturana, F., Tacconi, S., & Italiano, G. F. (2015). A machine learning-based approach to digital triage. In *Handbook of Digital Forensics of Multimedia Data and Devices* (pp. 94–132).

Marziale, L., Richard, G., & Roussev, V. (2007). Massive threading: using GPUs to increase the performance of digital forensics tools. *Digital Investigation, 4,* 73–81.

McKemmish, R. (1999). *What is forensic computing?.*

Mee, V., Tryfonas, T., & Sutherland, I. (2006). The Windows Registry as a forensic artefact: illustrating evidence collection for internet usage. *Digital Investigation, 3*(3), 166–173.

Nance, K., Hay, B., & Bishop, M. (2009). Digital forensics: defining a research agenda. In *42nd Hawaii International Conference on System Sciences, 2009. HICSS'09* (pp. 1–6). IEEE.

NIJ. (2004). *Forensic examination of digital evidence: a guide for law enforcement*, http://nij.gov/nij/pubs-sum/199408.htm.

Noel, G. E., & Peterson, G. L. (2014). Applicability of Latent Dirichlet Allocation to multi-disk search. *Digital Investigation, 11*(1), 43–56.

O'Connor, O. (2004). Deploying forensic tools via PXE. *Digital Investigation, 1*(3), 173–176.

Okolica, J. S., Peterson, G. L., & Mills, R. F. (2007). Using author topic to detect insider threats from email traffic. *Digital Investigation, 4*(3–4), 158–164.

Olsson, J., & Boldt, M. (2009). Computer forensic timeline visualization tool. *digital investigation, 6,* 78–87.

Overill, R. E., Silomon, J. A. M., & Roscoe, K. A. (2013). Triage template pipelines in digital forensic investigations. *Digital Investigation, 10*(2), 168–174.

Palmer, G. (2001). A road map for digital forensic research. In *Report From the First Digital Forensic Research Workshop (DFRWS)*, August 7–8, 2001.

Palmer, G. (2002). Forensic analysis in the digital world. *International Journal of Digital Evidence, 1*(1), 1–6.

Parashar, A., Paliwal, N., & Shelke, R. (2015). Cloud computing based forensic analysis for mobile applications using data mining. *International Journal of Advance Research in Computer Science and Management Studies, 3*(3), 319–325.

Parsonage, H. (2009). *Computer forensics case assessment and triage-some ideas for discussion*, Retrieved August 4, from http://computerforensics.parsonage.co.uk/triage/triage.htm.

Peisert, S., Bishop, M., & Marzullo, K. (2008). Computer forensics *in forensis. SIGOPS Operating Systems Review, 42*(3), 112–122.

Pollitt, M. M. (2013). Triage: A practical solution or admission of failure. *Digital Investigation, 10* (2), 87–88.

Pringle, N., & Burgess, M. (2014). Information assurance in a distributed forensic cluster. *Digital Investigation, 11*(Suppl. 1), S36–S44.

Pringle, N., & Sutherland, I. (2008). Is a computational grid a suitable platform for high performance digital forensics?. In *Proceedings of the 7th European Conference on Information Warfare and Security* (p. 175). Academic Conferences Limited.

Pyle, D. (1999). *Data preparation for data mining.* Morgan Kaufmann.

Quick, D., & Choo, K.-K. R. (2013). Dropbox analysis: Data remnants on user machines. *Digital Investigation, 10*(1), 3–18.

Quick, D., Martini, B., & Choo, K.-K.R. (2014). *Cloud storage forensics.* Syngress: An Imprint of Elsevier,

Quintana, M., Uribe, S., Sánchez, F., & Álvarez, F. (2015). Recommendation techniques in forensic data analysis: a new approach. In *2015 6th International Conference on Imaging for Crime Prevention and Detection (ICDP-15).*

Raghavan, S. (2013). Digital forensic research: current state of the art. *CSI Transactions on ICT, 1* (1), 91–114.

Reyes, A., Oshea, K., Steele, J., Hansen, J., Jean, B., & Ralph, T. (2007). *Digital forensics and analyzing data, Cyber Crime Investigations* (pp. 219–2590). Elsevier.

Richard, G., & Roussev, V. (2006a). Digital forensics tools: the next generation. *Digital Crime and Forensic Science in Cyberspace*, 75.

Richard, G., & Roussev, V. (2006b). Next-generation digital forensics. *Communications of the ACM, 49*(2), 76–80.

Riley, J. W., Dampier, D. A., & Vaughn, R. (2008). A comparison of forensic hard drive imagers: A time analysis comparison between the ICS image MASSter-Solo III and the logicube talon. *Journal of Digital Forensic Practice, 2*(2), 74–82.

Rockwell, M. (2015). *ICE unveils expanded cyber forensics lab,* 1105 Media, Inc., Retrieved July 23, from http://fcw.com/articles/2015/07/22/dhs-ice-expansion.aspx.

Rogers, M. K. (2004). The future of computer forensics: a needs analysis survey. *Computers & Security, 23*(1), 12–16.

Rogers, M. K., Goldman, J., Mislan, R., Wedge, T., & Debrota, S. (2006). Computer forensics field triage process model. In *Proceedings of the conference on Digital Forensics, Security and Law, 1*, 19–37.

Roussev, V., & Quates, C. (2012). Content triage with similarity digests: the M57 case study. *Digital Investigation, 9*, S60–S68.

Roussev, V., & Richard, G. (2004). Breaking the performance wall: the case for distributed digital forensics. In *Proceedings of the 2004 Digital Forensics Research Workshop.*

Roussev, V., Quates, C., & Martell, R. (2013). Real-time digital forensics and triage. *Digital Investigation, 10*(2), 158–167.

Schatz, B., & Clark, A. J. (2006). An open architecture for digital evidence integration. In *AusCERT Asia Pacific Information Technology Security Conference, May 21–26, 2006.*

Shannon, M. (2004). Forensic relative strength scoring: ASCII and entropy scoring. *International Journal of Digital Evidence, 2*(4), 151–169.

Shaw, A., & Browne, A. (2013). A practical and robust approach to coping with large volumes of data submitted for digital forensic examination. *Digital Investigation, 10*(2), 116–128.

Sheldon, A. (2005). The future of forensic computing. *Digital Investigation, 2*(1), 31–35.

Shiaeles, S., Chryssanthou, A., & Katos, V. (2013). On-scene triage open source forensic tool chests: Are they effective? *Digital Investigation, 10*(2), 99–115.

Sommer, P. (2004). The challenges of large computer evidence cases. *Digital Investigation, 1*(1), 16–17.

Stevens, M. W. (2004). Unification of relative time frames for digital forensics. *Digital Investigation, 1*(3), 225–239.

Stüttgen, J. (2011). *Selective imaging: Creating efficient forensic images by selecting content first.* Mannheim University.

Teelink, S., & Erbacher, R. (2006). Improving the computer forensic analysis process through visualization. *Communications of the ACM, 49*(2), 71–75.

Turnbull, B., & Randhawa, S. (2015). Automated event and social network extraction from digital evidence sources with ontological mapping. *Digital Investigation, 13,* 94–106.

Turnbull, B., Taylor, R., & Blundell, B. (2009). The Anatomy of electronic evidence; quantitative analysis of police E-Crime data. In *ARES'09. International Conference on Availability, Reliability and Security, 2009 (*143–149).

Turner, P. (2005). Unification of digital evidence from disparate sources (digital evidence bags). *Digital Investigation, 2*(3), 223–228.

Turner, P. (2006). Selective and intelligent imaging using digital evidence bags. *Digital Investigation, 3,* 59–64.

van Baar, R. B., van Beek, H. M. A., & van Eijk, E. J. (2014). Digital forensics as a service: A game changer. *Digital Investigation, 11*(Suppl. 1), S54–S62.

van Beek, H., van Eijk, E., van Baar, R., Ugen, M., Bodde, J., & Siemelink, A. (2015). Digital forensics as a service: Game on. *Digital Investigation, 15,* 20–38.

Vidas, T., Kaplan, B., & Geiger, M. (2014). OpenLV: empowering investigators and first-responders in the digital forensics process. *Digital Investigation, 11*(Suppl. 1), S45–S53.

Walmart. (2014). *Western digital green 4 TB desktop internal hard-drive*, Retrieved June 21, from http://www.walmart.com/ip/WD-Green-4TB-Desktop-Internal-Hard-Drive/30579528.

Walter, C. (2005). Kryder's law. *Scientific American, 293*(2), 32–33.

Wang, L., Lu, K., Liu, P., Ranjan, R., & Chen, L. (2014). IK-SVD: dictionary learning for spatial big data via incremental atom update. *Computing in Science & Engineering, 16*(4), 41–52.

Wang, L., Geng, H., Liu, P., Lu, K., Kolodziej, J., Ranjan, R., et al. (2015). Particle Swarm Optimization based dictionary learning for remote sensing big data. *Knowledge-Based Systems, 79,* 43–50.

Weiser, M., Biros, D. P., & Mosier, G. (2006). Development of a national repository of digital forensic intelligence. *Glenn S. Dardick, Editor-in-Chief Longwood University Virginia, USA* (p. 5).

Wiles, J., Alexander, T., Ashlock, S., Ballou, S., Depew, L., Dominguez, G., et al. (2007). Forensic examination in a terabyte world. *Techno Security's Guide to E-Discovery and Digital Forensics* (pp. 129–146). Elsevier.

Wong, A. (2010). Explosion of data envelops man in the street, *The Australian*, February 9, 2010.

Zimmerman, E. (2013). *Imaging test results*, Retrieved June 18, from https://docs.google.com/spreadsheet/lv?key=0Al7os14ND-cFdGp1NDR2WGwyakR2TkJtNUFXa29pNXc&type=view&gid=0&f=true&sortcolid=11&sortasc=true&rowsperpage=250.

Chapter 3
Data Reduction and Data Mining Frame-Work

As highlighted in Chap. 2, there is a need for a methodology and framework for data reduction and data mining of digital forensic data. This chapter outlines the digital forensic data reduction and data mining framework, which endeavours to expand the process used for traditional forensic computer analysis to include data reduction, data mining, and input from external source data. This serves to expand common digital forensic frameworks, to be applicable when dealing with a large volume of digital forensic data.

As discussed in the preceding chapter, the increase in digital evidence presented for analysis to digital forensic laboratories has been an issue for many years, leading to lengthy backlogs of work (Justice 2016; Parsonage 2009). This is compounded with the growing size of storage devices (Garfinkel 2010). The increasing volume of data has been discussed by various digital forensic scholars and practitioners such as McKemmish (1999) and Raghavan et al. (2009). Whilst many of the challenges posed by the volume of data are addressed in part by new developments in technology, the underlying issue has not been adequately resolved.

As outlined in Chap. 2, over many years, there have been a variety of different ideas put forward in relation to addressing the increasing volume of data;

- data mining (Beebe 2009; Beebe and Clark 2005; Brown et al. 2005; Huang et al. 2010; Palmer 2001; Shannon 2004),
- data reduction (Beebe 2009; Ferraro and Russell 2004; Garfinkel 2006b; Greiner 2009; Kenneally and Brown 2005; Pollitt 2013; Raghavan 2013; Turner 2007),
- triage (Garfinkel 2010; Parsonage 2009; Reyes et al. 2007; Shiaeles et al. 2013; Vidas et al. 2014),
- cross-drive analysis (Garfinkel 2010; Raghavan et al. 2009),

---

Material presented in this chapter is based on the following publication:

Quick, D. and K.-K.R. Choo, Data Reduction and Data Mining Framework for Digital Forensic Evidence: Storage, Intelligence, Review and Archive. Trends and Issues in Crime and Criminal Justice, 2014. 480: p. 1–11.

- user profiling (Abraham 2006; Garfinkel 2010),
- parallel and distributed processing (Lee et al. 2008; Nance et al. 2009; Pringle and Sutherland 2008; Roussev and Richard 2004),
- graphic processing units (Marziale et al. 2007; Richard and Roussev 2006),
- intelligence analysis techniques (Beebe 2009),
- Digital Forensics as a Service (Alink et al. 2006; Bhoedjang et al. 2012; van Baar et al. 2014).
- artificial intelligence (Hoelz et al. 2009; Sheldon 2005), and
- visualisation (Teelink and Erbacher 2006).

Despite there being much discussion regarding the data volume challenge and many calls for research into the applications of data mining and other techniques to address the problem, there has been very little published work in relation to a method or framework to apply data mining techniques or other methods to reduce and analyse the increasing volume of data. Of these, data reduction has potentially the greatest influence across the various stages of digital forensic analysis, as it can enable rapid collection, preservation, and analysis of data.

In addition, the value of extracting or using intelligence from digital forensic data has not been discussed, nor has there been any research regarding the use of open, closed and confidential source information during digital forensic analysis. A reliable and real-world applicable digital forensic data reduction method will also assist with the improved use of forensic intelligence, in that digital forensic data can be stored in vastly smaller subsets and assist with this forensic data being used for investigation and/or intelligence purposes.

In this chapter, a data reduction and data mining framework is proposed that incorporates a process of reducing data volume by focusing on a subset of information. This process is not designed to replace full analysis, but provide a method of focusing an investigation to review items of importance, reduce data storage requirements for archival and retrieval purposes, and provide a capability to undertake intelligence analysis of digital forensic data. Full analysis of digital evidence may still be necessary and the proposed framework outlined in this chapter serves to support analysis rather than replace it.

The framework provides the capability to conduct a review of a subset of data as a triage process and to store subset data for intelligence analysis, research, archival and historical review purposes.

3.1 Motivation

The next section explains the challenges (primarily costs) in storing evidential data, which highlights the need for a cost-efficient data reduction process. The proposed data reduction and data mining framework is then presented, alongside an explanation of how it can be applied, as well as its benefits. The *Pilot study* section

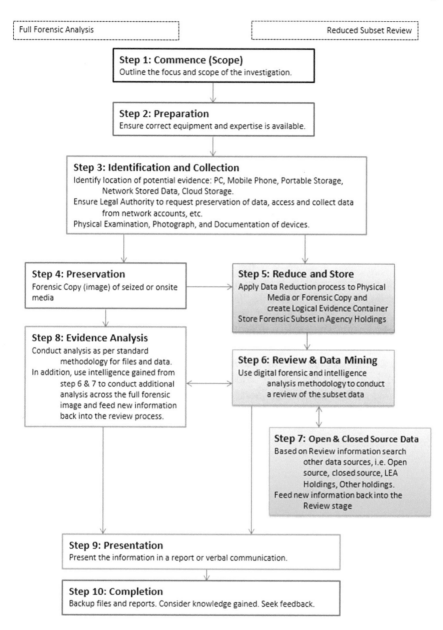

Fig. 3.1 Digital forensic data reduction and data mining framework

outlines the results of initial research examining the data reduction and triage potential relating to Step 5 and Step 6 of the proposed framework (see Fig. 3.1).

The issue of the volume of data required to be analysed in a digital forensic examination has been raised over many years. McKemmish (1999) stated that the rapid increase in the size of storage media is probably the greatest single challenge to forensic analysis. In the interim years, there have been many publications stating the increasing volume of data is a major issue for forensic analysis. However, there have been no overall solutions proposed and the problem is still discussed.

Alzaabi et al. (2013) discuss the ongoing trend of storage capacity increasing and the prices of devices decreasing, and while there are tools and techniques to assist an investigator, the time and effort to undertake analysis remains a serious challenge. For example, Raghavan (2013, p. 91) states that the 'exponential growth of technology has also brought with it some serious challenges for digital forensic research' and suggests that this is the 'single largest challenge to conquer' Raghavan (2013, p. 108). When discussing the challenges posed to the field of digital forensics, Dr Eugene Spafford (cited in Palmer 2001, p. 7) stated that, "*[d] igital technology continues to change rapidly. Terabyte disks and decreasing time to market are but two symptoms that cause investigators difficulty in applying currently available analytical tools.*"

Also highlighted in Chap. 2 is the comparison of Moore's Law and Kryder's Law. While storage capacity is doubling every year, the capacity to process data is only doubling every 18–24 months, leading to an ever-growing gap in the capability to process the volume of data seized using processing power alone. Commercial forensic software companies have changed the underlying methods of storing and processing information, and have introduced some parallel and distributed processing options for their forensic analysis software, although; as the size of digital forensic investigations continues to increase, current tools still take considerable time to process the increasing volume of data (Marziale et al. 2007). Apache Solr and Elastic Elasticsearch are two products that readily scale out, but until digital forensic software indexing tools incorporate this functionality when dealing with increasingly larger images of hard drives and include an ability to process the atypical complex data according to the disparate data types prior to indexing, the time to process digital forensic data will continue to increase as the volume of seized data increases.

In the literature review (Chap. 2) the information from the FBI RCFL annual reports as summarised in Table 2.2, directly shows the growth in digital forensic data volume (FBI_RCFL 2003–2012). The figures show an increase in the volume of data analysed each year, growing from 82 terabytes (TB) in fiscal year 2003–5,986 TB (5.8 petabytes (PB)), an overall increase of an average of 67 and 36% per annum average increase for the last five fiscal years.

Using the total volume of forensic data examined by the FBI RCFL of 20 PB (from Table 2.2) as a baseline figure for calculations, the cost to store this volume of data uncompressed in a manner that is readily accessible is expensive. In 2011, to house 14 PB of data, a commercial solution that had the ability to scale to 15 PB cost an estimated US$18 m (Giri 2012; Suleman 2011).

A cheaper option is to store the data using widely available 3 TB removable hard drives, with the estimated cost of hard drives alone being US$922,292 (2013 figures). This consists of 6,588 external hard disk drives purchased for US$139.99 from a consumer electronics store (Best_Buy 2013). However, the forensic data would be archived and not available for immediate review. Tape storage or other solutions would potentially be cheaper, but also require a method to retrieve the data from the stored medium prior to enabling access to the data for processing or searching. Consequently, the data is not readily available for review or analysis.

Forensic bit-for-bit copies of hard drives or other media (commonly referred to as forensic 'images') are often compressed, using containers such as the Expert Witness, E01, or other compressed formats. Data analysis was conducted on the figures for the volume of data comprising a range of forensic case types examined by the South Australia Police (SAPOL) Electronic Crime Section (ECS). The data examined for 43 cases involving 107 evidence items compared the size of the original media with the subsequent size of compressed E01 files. It was determined that the compression amount varied according to the data on each evidence item and ranged from 92 percent to two percent of the total volume. The average compression observed across 107 hard drives was 51.1%. When this compression percentage is applied to the FBI's 20 PB of data, this reduces the storage requirement to just over 10 PB of forensic images. Hence, using the compressed forensic image format would reduce the cost to store the data.

Even with the price of consumer grade hard drives and storage dropping, i.e. at a price point of $535[1] for a 10 TB consumer level hard disk drive, the need for enterprise-level storage reliability means there remains an increased cost to agencies, and when scaled upwards above 100 TB the cost can significantly increase, usually with a trade-off between volume, speed, and reliability. In conjunction with the constrained economic environment, annual ongoing purchases of additional storage may not be a viable option for many agencies. Hence, there is a need for alternative method to a requirement of an ongoing purchase of increasingly larger volumes of storage.

To summarise, it would be very costly to store the entire volume of digital forensic data examined by the FBI, either in an archived or accessible format. As discussed by Garfinkel (2006a), government and law enforcement agencies rarely store or archive forensic copies, which limits cross drive analysis capability. Storing or archiving forensic data, such as on networked storage solutions, is beneficial; however, the rapidly increasing volume of data requires ever expanding network storage volumes, with the associated costs.

Whilst some agencies routinely archive important data, there is no published resource detailing what is 'important data' and hence should be retained, and anecdotal information is that many agencies do not routinely archive any data. Surprisingly in some agencies, all data is destroyed when a case is completed through Court. This highlights a need for a method to identify what data is important and should be archived, and a need to reduce the volume of data for archival purposes.

Of the agencies that do archive case data, it is often stored on optical media (CD or DVD) or tape backup, and sent to national archive storage. The process for

---

[1]https://www.engadget.com/2016/07/19/seagate-unveils-a-10tb-hard-drive-for-your-home-pc/.

practitioners to gain access to the off-site stored archives can involve the time to complete paperwork to locate and order the archived material, and then wait for possibly days or weeks to have the archived data delivered then transfer the stored medium to accessible storage for processing and analysis. The ability to have a subset of pre-identified data which is readily accessible with much less data storage requirements will enable an improved ability to undertake cross case analysis of historical data without additional cost to an agency (time and money). This highlights a need for a process to reduce the volume of data to that which is potentially relevant.

The growth in volume and number of devices impacts forensic examinations in many ways, including increasing lengths of time to create forensic copies and conduct analysis, which contributes to the increase in the backlog of requests. Digital forensic practitioners, especially those in government and law enforcement agencies, will continue to be under pressure to deliver more with less especially in today's economic landscape.

This gives rise to a variety of needs, including:

- A more efficient method of collecting and preserving evidence.
- A capacity to triage evidence prior to conducting full analysis.
- Reduced data storage requirements.
- An ability to conduct a review of information in a timely manner for intelligence, research and evidential purposes.
- An ability to archive important data.
- An ability to quickly retrieve and review archived data.
- A source of data to enable a review of current and historical cases (intelligence, research and knowledge management).

There is an opportunity to consider methods to reduce the volume of data at each stage of the forensic analysis process in relation to the seven needs listed in the chapter introduction, namely faster collection, reduced storage, timely review, intelligence, research, knowledge management, archive and retrieval. Consideration can be given to the type of data collected, stored and reviewed, with a focus on data that will provide the greatest information. Kenneally and Brown (2005) outlined a process for selective imaging to address the risks associated with collecting full forensic images for large drives, primarily the cost in time and resources, by selecting which data to image at the collection stage. The legal standards of reasonableness and relevance are raised to address concerns in relation to not undertaking analysis of a full forensic image. However, it could be argued that as the difference relates to hours or days, in a criminal or civil arena, it could be deemed reasonable to take a full bit-for-bit image and conduct analysis with all available and potentially relevant data. Hence, the proposed framework (see Fig. 3.1) retains full imaging and analysis steps, with the reduced collection and review steps included to assist and support full analysis, rather than replace it.

Beebe (2009) proposed that a solution to the volume of data challenge is to strategically select a subset of data rather than an entire bitstream copy and that the subset could include portions of unallocated space. However, it was stated that further research is needed to determine the exact process to be undertaken.

As an example of potential subset data; files such as Microsoft Windows Internet Explorer Internet history 'index.dat' files and other browser history files and folders, can provide a great volume of information in a smaller size, when compared with other data, such as unallocated clusters, or 'Pagefile.sys' memory paging files.

Hence, collecting and storing Internet history files and not collecting or storing unallocated clusters, can reduce storage requirements and still retain information that is potentially important to an investigation. There are many file types of importance such as Log Files, Windows Registry Files, Windows Desktop Search database files, Prefetch files, email archival files and Word documents. The reduction process is undertaken on the understanding that by not collecting or storing all data, there is a subsequent risk that evidential information is potentially missed and therefore a subset of data may not be suitable for full or thorough analysis.

Turner (2005) introduced the concept of Digital Evidence Bags as a method to store a variety of digital evidence while retaining information relating to the source and location of the data subset. Schatz and Clark (2006) introduced the concept of a Sealed Digital Evidence Bag, providing for referencing between evidence bags. However, commercial forensic software such as EnCase, FTK, and X-Ways, provide the capability of selectively imaging files to support the collection of subset data into logical evidence files.

Garfinkel (2006b) discusses Forensic Feature Extraction (FFE) and Cross Drive Analysis methods. FFE is outlined as a scan of a disk image for email addresses, message information, date and time information, cookies, social security and credit card numbers. The information from the data scan is stored as XML for analysis and comparison. However, as the original data is interpreted, there may be instances where new techniques are difficult to apply to the original or historical data. There have been many developments in recent years whereby additional information is able to be extracted from data holdings that were previously unknown. For example, Windows Registry analysis methodologies include newly discovered areas for locating information (Carvey 2011).

The following proposed Digital Forensic Data Reduction and Data Mining Framework focuses on collecting and storing original files so that any future ability to extract information from data is retained (as the original file is retained and can be reprocessed with new methodologies or tools). The FFE and Cross Drive Analysis processes are valid and provide benefits based on current knowledge and capabilities. However, storing the original files should be undertaken where possible in an effort to future-proof data holdings, which could even lead to cold-case style analysis of historical cases with new techniques or methodologies.

3.2   Proposed Digital Forensic Data Reduction and Data Mining Framework

The proposed Digital Forensic Data Reduction and Data Mining Framework (Fig. 3.1) applies to various stages of a digital forensic examination. This does not replace the need for full analysis and the framework is mapped to a common digital forensic framework with breakout steps for the reduction and review stages to maintain the distinction between full analysis and the data reduction and review steps (see Fig. 3.1). This builds on a common digital forensic framework, listed on the left side of the framework, with the reduction and review steps highlighted on the right side. Current digital forensic frameworks (ACPO 2006; McKemmish 1999; NIJ 2004, 2008) have a focus on conducting thorough analysis for evidence, which as outlined above, is not replaced with this framework. The steps are aligned with the digital forensic framework of Quick and Choo (2013a), an extension of the framework of McKemmish (1999), merged with the intelligence analysis cycle (see Ratcliffe 2003).

The following outlines the steps of the proposed Digital Forensic Data Reduction and Data Mining Framework (Fig. 3.1);

Step 1—Commence (Scope)

The first step in the framework serves to outline the scope of the inquiry, including background information, analysis requirements and other information. This is common to other digital forensic frameworks, and is not altered in the reduction framework. (See Quick and Choo 2013a).

Step 2—Preparation

This second step of the framework is again a common one and exists to ensure the correct equipment and expertise is available. Again, this step is not altered from common frameworks.

Step 3—Identification and Collection

The third step of the framework is the process of identifying the location of potential evidence, such as a personal computer, hard drive, mobile phone, portable storage, network stored data, or cloud storage. This is undertaken with appropriate legal authority to collect media containing potential evidence. This step can also include the physical examination of devices and documentation of media, including source location, time and date accuracy. This step is not altered from common frameworks.

Step 4—Preservation

This step relates to the preservation of evidence and includes the process of making a full forensic bit-for-bit copy (image) of write-blocked media and data using common forensic tools appropriate for the task, such as Guidance Software EnCase, X-Ways Forensic, or AccessData FTK Imager. If a physical examination has not occurred, this would be the first part of this step to ensure information about the source of the evidence is documented. This step is not outlined in depth as it is common to standard frameworks.

Step 5—Reduce and Store

This is a proposed new step that can be undertaken prior to, at the same time as, or subsequent to, the preservation of evidence (Step 4). Step 5, the reduction process, is undertaken on the understanding that common forensic rules and practices are complied with, namely no change to the original media is made where possible (ACPO 2006). If changes to media are suspected to result from the subset reduction collection process, this should either not be undertaken, or be done subsequent to the evidence preservation process to ensure the evidence is not put at risk of not being accepted in court due to any changes made. The subset reduction process can be run across the original (write-blocked) media, or a full forensic image. Chapter 4 relates to a detailed discussion outlining the proposed data reduction process, Data Reduction by Selective Imaging (DRbSI), and the research results.

When working with electronic evidence, there is a potential to inadvertently change original data if agency or other guidelines such as ACPO (2006) are not adhered to. Hence, forensic guidelines need to be adhered to at all stages. The reduction process should not be undertaken to the detriment of the preservation process and hence, evidential and legal requirements take priority. Examiners must adhere to current best practice in relation to electronic evidence to ensure evidence is not at risk of not being accepted in court. However, examiners are not the only impacting factor in relation to acceptance of evidence in court. In *Roman and Anor v Commonwealth of Australia and Ors* [2004] NTSC 9 (11 March 2004), it is reported that the investigating officer spent an hour looking through a tower computer, which was subsequently seized and analysed. In *R v Ravindran* (No. 4) [2013] NSWSC 1106 (15 August 2013), the actions of the seizing member potentially affected the analysis of a computer, but not the acceptance of the evidence.

The reduction process should be undertaken in a forensically sound manner using hardware or software write blockers and forensic software to enable the collection of data subsets. As an example; connecting a SATA hard drive via a hardware write blocker to ensure data is not altered. Forensic software is then used to access the write-protected hard drive and pre-built conditions or filters used to display and select files containing potential data of interest, such as Windows Registry files, Internet browsing history, log files, documents, software initialisation files, software data files and other files of importance. The files of interest are selected and then preserved in a logical evidence container (L01, AD1, or CTR). By focusing on files of importance rather than copying every bit of a hard drive, it is possible to substantially reduce the size of data preserved (see Chap. 4 for reduction figures observed).

While the reduction process will not alleviate the need to image everything in every case, there is a potential to speed up the overall process and reduce the need to image and store full forensic copies of every item seized. In practice, a triage process using a data subset to identify which items contain potential evidence can potentially reduce the need to image everything. While this process may initially identify data or evidence relevant to a case, there may still be a need to fully image and conduct analysis of a full forensic copy (depending on investigation scope). A great benefit of using the data reduction by selective imaging approach is that if items are identified at the triage stage with potential evidence, this may alleviate the need to image everything. Collecting a data subset and undertaking a rapid review may identify evidence on an item, allowing an examiner to produce a report and supply this to investigators or legal counsel and not require full forensic imaging and analysis of every item seized.

In addition, to gain the greatest benefit from data mining and intelligence analysis across disparate cases, there is a need to collect similar data across cases. The process undertaken in the pilot study (outlined in the next section) included analysis of a digital forensic corpus and real world data to identify files with potential to provide the greatest information and exclude files with the least potential to provide information. Once the files with the greatest potential were identified, a filtering process was applied to a variety of cases and investigations types to collect the same or similar data from a variety of cases. This is further explored in Chap. 4 in relation to a more detailed collection regime, and Volume 2 in relation to rapid analysis, and potential intelligence.

In practice, a data subset should be collected from each item in a case where there are multiple items (even if not analysed) and then archived. This can then assist with any future questions that may arise about digital forensic data holdings, such as questions from prosecution or legal counsel prior to court proceedings.

The benefits of the reduction process will potentially be greatest when the original exhibit has been seized and can be imaged at a later stage (if required). In a situation where an item cannot be seized, there is still a potential need to take a full forensic copy. The reduction process can be of benefit prior to undertaking analysis, as a subset can be quickly copied from the forensic copy or source media and undertake a review to determine if the item has potential evidence. The subset reduction process can also be used onsite to determine if an item contains potential evidence and assist in making a decision to seize or not.

Cloud storage provides users with an ability to store large amounts of data in remotely accessible storage locations (Quick and Choo 2013a, b, 2014). This can cause issues for an examiner in relation to identifying the data, collecting the data, and analysing the data (Quick and Choo 2013c; Quick et al. 2014). A review of a data subset from a computer or hard drive can potentially identify cloud stored data faster than waiting for a full forensic image to complete and process (indexing, metadata extraction and other processes).

There are a range of issues relating to the collection of data from cloud storage including legal issues, the time to access and preserve the data, and undertaking analysis of the preserved data. Collecting a data subset from cloud storage has potential time and storage size savings. This can be achieved by collecting the data with potential to provide evidence, rather than collecting every byte of data stored remotely. Conducting a review of a subset of data will also be faster than under-taking a review of a full forensic copy. However, the needs of an investigation may dictate the need to collect and preserve every byte of data stored remotely and undertake full analysis.

It is also possible to apply a reduction framework to mobile phones or tablet computers; for example, using the option to only save call-related data, internet history, email and other software data files, with large files such as pictures and video not saved within a reduced subset (a full extract collection would be first undertaken for evidential analysis purposes). This is discussed in Volume 2 in relation to a reduction method applicable for portable devices.

As part of the reduction process outlined in Chap. 4, video files can be converted to thumbnail snapshots for review purposes. As an example, software that takes consecutive interval snapshots of video frames can be used, whereby the storage requirements are vastly reduced.

The data subset files can also be stored with other data subset files; for example, in a structured manner in folder and sub-folders as per the work request number, by financial year, case number allocation, exhibit number or device information. As the reduced data subsets are vastly smaller than full forensic images, it is possible to store a considerable number of subset logical containers in a comparatively small storage space. The resulting subset files can then be reviewed for relevant information (as addressed in Step 6 outlined in Volume 2).

The process of Data Reduction by Selective Imaging (DRbSI) is discussed in Chap. 4 and achieved dramatic reductions in data volume from digital forensic source data holdings.

Step 6—Review and Data Mining

The next step (detailed in Volume 2) is a review of the DRbSI data subset which is conducted using the smaller subset of data from Step 5. As the data is substantially reduced, the time to process and review can be dramatically faster. The process used for undertaking forensic analysis (Bunting and Wei 2006; Carrier 2005; Casey 2011) can be used with the smaller subset of data and results in a faster review of the information (see Volume 2 for test data experiment and real world application findings). The information review can consist of analysis of internet browsing history, filename information, a timeline review, Windows Registry analysis, keyword indexing and searching, hash analysis and other common forensic analysis techniques using a range of tools. Volume 2 outlines the proposed process of Quick Analysis which is discussed in depth.

The ability to index forensic data prior to analysis has been available for many years. However, with the ever-growing size of data, the time to index the data is also growing. This is leading to longer times an examiner has to wait until the indexing is complete. The process of indexing by its very nature does not fully index every character or word and hence, searches undertaken across an index can potentially miss important evidence when compared with a full text search. By indexing a data subset, rather than the entire forensic image, there will be potential time savings in relation to processing and indexing (see Pilot study in the next section, and further experiments and findings in Volume 2).

In addition, using the subset data for intelligence analysis and research of trends is an area that can provide substantial information to assist current and future investigations. Using an intelligence analysis methodology (as documented in a range of publications such as (UNODC 2011) and Quarnby and Young 2010) can assist to formalise the review process. When applying intelligence analysis practices to digital forensic data, expertise in relation to digital forensic analysis is beneficial to understand the relevance of information and to be able to extract meaningful inferences and hypotheses from the observed data.

As discussed in the literature review (Chap. 2) the potential intelligence to be gained from digital forensic data holdings is an area that is infrequently discussed in academic literature. However, there are vast potential gains to be made from undertaking analysis of these holdings for intelligence rather than just evidential purposes. Potential information can include names, addresses, vehicles, telephone numbers, associates and email correspondence. It is also possible for a psychological profile of the user to be built using the information stored within a user's computer or mobile device, such as common websites and interests of the user. This can potentially be determined from a variety of sources on a computer or mobile device, such as internet history, bookmarks, recent files viewed or multimedia played and a range of other intelligence.

There is also a potential to conduct analysis across a range of disparate investigations for common linkages, further providing valuable intelligence or evidence to assist in investigations and prosecutions. Additionally, researching trends over time can assist to provide information to investigators as part of focusing investigations to locate evidence earlier. For example, research of historical case data may highlight a trend showing the increased use of specific internet chat software among specific criminal offenders and as such, future investigations can first look for these data remnants rather than examining data from software that has declining use.

To undertake any use of collected data, an examiner must ensure they abide by all legal authorities relating to the collection and use of seized data. There must be legal authority to collect data and also examine data, and in particular, use the data for mining or analysis purposes. Anyone accessing the seized data, whether it is a full forensic copy or data subset, must ensure they have the legal authority to do so.

At this stage of the framework the subset data is reviewed and the findings can be utilised with other information (such as Step 7 further outlined in Volume 2) to provide information for evidential analysis (Step 8). Data can also be classified according to reliability and security, as per common intelligence practice (UNODC 2011).

A process of Digital Forensic Quick Analysis is discussed in Volume 2 and achieved analysis of subsets and full forensic images in reduced timeframes. The data mining aspect of this step is outlined in relation to examining mobile devices, and semi-automated data mining of information across devices and cases is explored.

Step 7—Open and Closed Source Data

The information and intelligence gained from the analysis and review of DRbSI subsets (Step 5 and 6) can be used to further search other information sources, such as open and closed source data (Step 7). The research into this aspect of the framework is detailed in Volume 2. Closed source data can include confidential internal reports and other information holdings. Open source data includes information gathered from internet sources such as publicly available Facebook information, Twitter data, media reports, and Weblogs (blogs). The information gained from external sources and the Review stage can then be used to provide input back to the Evidence Analysis Step (Step 8) which serves to further increase the knowledge base used to determine information of evidential value, or of relevance to an investigation.

A process of Digital Forensic Intelligence and Open Source Intelligence (DFINT +OSINT) is discussed in Volume 2 along with research findings which details the method researched as part of this book, and achieved a fusion of intelligence from DRbSI subsets and open source information to enhance digital forensic data holdings.

Step 8—Evidence Analysis

This step is common to digital forensic analysis and previously documented (Bunting and Wei 2006; Carrier 2005; Casey 2011). Evidence analysis is conducted as per standard methodology for files and data. However, in this proposed framework, if information or evidence is discovered during the Review stage (Step 6), this may answer all investigation questions as outlined in the Scope (Step 1), and alleviate the need to undertake full analysis. In addition, the information gained from conducting the review (Step 6) and other source data (Step 7) can be used when conducting analysis of the full forensic image to locate data relating to an investigation, which may result in additional information being discovered, feeding back into the Review and External Source data stages (Steps 6 and 7). The process of Quick Analysis as outlined in Volume 2 includes an ability to apply analytical methods to DRbSI reduced data subsets or full forensic images, and is also applicable to this stage of the framework.

Evidential analysis can be undertaken to confirm the findings from the review of the subset data and to locate additional data of importance. Any additional data (not present in the subset files) can be preserved in a logical evidence container and included with the reduced subset store for archive or historical review. The process of Digital Forensic Quick Analysis as discussed in Volume 2 is applicable to full forensic analysis, and the process is outlined, along with research findings which examine the proposed method, and achieved analysis of subsets and full forensic images in reduced timeframes.

Step 9—Presentation

At this stage of the framework, the findings of evidence analysis are compiled. This can be in a written report format, or a verbal communication with investigators, legal counsel and a formal presentation of evidence to a Court. In addition, intelligence and other findings from the Review step can be disseminated as per the intelligence analysis process (UNODC 2011). Research findings can be communicated through academic or agency specific channels. The process of presentation is standard within common forensic frameworks, and is not discussed in depth, although attention is drawn to Chap. 4 which outlines the data reduction process in relation to the process of converting video to thumbnails has benefit to not only data reduction, but to presentation needs as well.

Step 10—Completion

The final stage of the proposed framework is to complete the examination. This is done to ensure all questions have been answered and feedback is sought from those involved, such as investigators and legal counsel. It is also important to provide feedback to those involved in the investigation to ensure they are aware of the completion of the matter, and their role in the process is recognized. At this stage, considerations are made in relation to initiating new investigations or inquiries. In addition, it is important to ensure all relevant files are backed up.

The proposed Digital Forensic Data Reduction Framework (Fig. 3.1) is used to guide the process of this research. Steps 1–4 are common forensic processes, and are not examined in this research.

The Data Reduction stage, Step 5 is outlined in the next section and the explored in detail in Chap. 4. Following this, the Review and Mining processes are outlined in Volume 2, and explored in detail, Including the process of Quick Analysis as applied to DRbSI subsets and full forensic images, advanced analysis using the DRbSI subsets, and the potential to gain intelligence from the DRbSI subsets in relation to mobile device forensic extracts. Step 7 is discussed, which examines the fusion of digital forensic data and open source information.

Steps 9 and 10 are common digital forensic procedures and are not examined in detail in this research.

3.3   Pilot Study Preliminary Findings

In the design process of the proposed framework, a pilot study was undertaken in relation to the data reduction process (Step 5 of Fig. 3.1) and applied to test data and real world digital forensic cases, which provided for a significant reduction in data storage and archive requirements.

The proposed reduction process (see Chap. 4 for further detail) was applied to the forensic disk copies comprising the Digital Corpora (Garfinkel et al. 2009). The results are listed in Table 3.1. To highlight the figures in the Corpora (Table 3.1), it can be seen that in the 'nps-2009-domexusers' case, the source data was a 40 GB hard drive (HD), the full forensic image (E01) file was 4 GB (10%), and the resulting DRbSI data subset was 84 MB (L01) representing 0.21% of the source volume. The 'nps-2011-scenario1' disk image is of a 74.5 GB hard drive, the full forensic image was 34.5 GB (46%), with the resulting DRbSI data subset was a 613 MB L01 file (0.82%).

Using South Australia Police (SAPOL) Electronic Crime Section (ECS) case files the proposed data reduction process was applied to a sample of full forensic images (see Table 3.2). The subsequent size of the reduced dataset files (L01 in Table 3.2) was then compared to the size of the full forensic copy (E01 in Table 3.2) and the original source media volume size (HD in Table 3.2). Across a sample range of 34 cases from financial years 2012 and 2013 (i.e. 1 July 2011–30

Table 3.1 Data reduction framework applied to digital corpora forensic images (Garfinkel et al. 2009)

Item	HD (in GB)	E01 (in GB)	L01 (in GB)	E01: HD ratio (%)	L01: E01 ratio (%)	L01: HD ratio (%)
2008 m57 Jean	10	2.83	0.088	28	3.11	0.88
4Dell Latitude	4.5	1	0.0735	22	7.35	1.63
charlie-2009-11-12	9.5	3.02	0.185	32	6.13	1.95
charlie-work-usb-2009-12-11	1	0.00883	0.0047	1	53.23	0.47
jo-2009-11-12	12	3.06	0.0971	26	3.17	0.81
jo-2009-12-11-002	14.3	5.53	0.312	39	5.64	2.18
nps-2009-domexusers	40	4	0.084	10	2.10	0.21
nps-2011-scenariol	74.5	34.5	0.613	46	1.78	0.82
nps-201 1-scenario4	232.8	18.1	0.668	8	3.69	0.29
pat-2009-12-11	12.1	2.97	0.243	25	8.18	2.01
terry-2009-12-11-001	19.1	7	0.157	37%	2.24	0.82
tracy-external-2012-07-03-initl	13.2	3.47	0.000518	26	0.01	0.00
tracy-home-2012-07-03-initial	17.4	3.99	0.605	23	15.16	3.48
tracy-home-2012-07-16-final	17.4	3.99	0.471	23	11.80	2.71
Total	477.80	93.47	3.60	19.56	3.85	0.75
Average	34.13	6.68	0.26	19.57	3.89	0.76

Table 3.2 Data reduction framework applied to SAPOL ECS cases

Item	No of drives	HD (in GB)	E01 (in GB)	L01 (in GB)	E01:HD ratio (%)	L01:E01 ratio (%)	L01:HD ratio (%)
Smallest	1	40	4.5	0.0415	11	0.92	0.10
Largest	1	1000	121	0.0143	12	0.12	0.01
Total (all cases)	212	102366.5					
E0l	107	45388	22040.68		51.1		
L0l	144	66438.5		62.98			0.196
E0l and L0l	37	9430	5197.9	22	55	0.423	0.233
Average (across all)		461.4	136.76	0.44	58.7	0.705	0.196

June 2013) comprising 144 hard drives and other media, the volume of data was able to be reduced to 0.196% of total evidence drive volume.

Whilst these figures differ from the figures from the test data corpus files, this can be explained in that many of the Corpora images are scenarios purposely built on smaller hard disk drives in a test environment, rather than larger hard drives observed in actual cases. As an example, one of the SAPOL ECS cases comprised

6 TB of hard drives, which when forensically imaged comprised 3 TB of E01 forensic copies (50%), and when the DRbSI data reduction process was used, reduced to 1.6 GB of L01 data subset files (0.03% of source data volume).

Applying the reduction percentage observed from the SAPOL ECS hard drives, the 20 PB FBI data volume discussed in the earlier section could be reduced to a much smaller subset of the data comprising the cases from 2003 to 2012. The potential storage cost savings could be quite significant and the ability to search the data would be considerably faster (resulting in more savings).

Also observed were benefits in conducting a quick review process (Step 6) by initially collecting a reduced subset and conducting a review while waiting for the full forensic image to complete. Results observed included a subset collection only taking 79 s to collect the reduced dataset from a 320 GB hard drive (Windows 7 Professional), compared with three hours to complete a full forensic copy and another three hours to verify the copy. Using EnCase 7.08 forensic software to process and fully index the reduced subset only took two minutes 53 s, compared with nearly six hours to process and index the full forensic copy. In relation to the storage requirements, the E01 images comprised 218 GB compared with 687 MB for the L01 file (0.215% L01:HD).

A review of the 687 MB DRbSI subset data located information of relevance in the internet history and the registry files (website listings and recent document entries), highlighting the need to conduct further analysis of the full forensic disk image. Had there been no information found in the review, the drive would still have been fully examined, but would have been undertaken subsequent to other items of a higher priority in the investigation.

When applied in a triage manner, the Digital Forensic Data Reduction and Data Mining Framework can enable rapid collection, processing, indexing and searching of subset data to take place, which can quickly highlight devices that contain potential evidential material. Other devices can be then excluded or given a lower priority if there is less chance of evidential data being present.

During the review of the DRbSI data, it was also observed there was information that can be utilised for intelligence purposes (Step 6, Data Mining), including the internet history of the user, documents authored by the user (e.g. resume information detailing the person's work history and experience, and email communication with associates) and other information that would be relevant for intelligence purposes. This data would also be of potential use for researching trends over time, such as specific websites visited in relation to alleged offence typologies.

Long-term storage of the reduced subset of data could also prove to be of benefit, as important data in its original format can be retained. If questions arise from investigators, prosecutors and counsel (which can often be many months after the analysis is finalised), it can be beneficial to be able to access the case subset data, such as registry files or internet history, to promptly answer questions relating to user accounts, recent documents, or browsing history, without having to fully reimage or reprocess physical evidence to enable analysis of the information.

It is also possible to examine many subset data cases by loading them into forensic software and reviewing data across a range of cases. An example is loading multiple mobile phone subset datasets (without pictures or videos) into visualisation software such as Intella, NUIX, or i2 Analyst Notebook, and use visualisations to locate links between disparate devices and cases.

While the reduced subset does not store all data and hence, may not be as comprehensive for full evidential analysis, the pilot study demonstrated the process serves a need for rapid review, analysis, triage, intelligence, research, and knowledge management purposes. Consider that data subsets of cases and devices examined could potentially be stored on relatively small hard drives or network storage. The reduction process provides the ability to search this data quite rapidly (when compared with a potential cost of storing full forensic images and the amount of time it would take to search potentially many petabytes of data). There is potential intelligence and evidential benefits in relation to an understanding of historical cases, such as the use of a particular URL across historical investigations, or matching illicit file hash values among disparate and historical cases, potentially providing valuable intelligence.

The Digital Forensic Data Reduction and Data Mining Framework can be applied as either an addition to an evidence analysis process to gain a faster understanding of information as a triage process or be considered for archival storage, cross-case knowledge, research and intelligence review benefits.

3.4   Discussion

The growth in digital forensic data has been ongoing for many years and with the predicted ongoing growth in technology and storage, is estimated to become increasingly larger over the coming years. This has led to large backlogs of evidence awaiting analysis. By utilising the Digital Forensic Data Reduction and Data Mining Framework and a reduced subset of data, a better understanding of data can be made at a substantially reduced cost, by comparison with storing full forensic images.

The data reduction subset process can be used to triage devices and media to quickly assess which devices may contain potential evidence and hence should be examined as a priority, and which devices have less potential evidence and can be given a lower priority for full analysis.

The findings of the pilot study have demonstrated that there are potential major benefits in the areas of data storage, as well as dramatic reductions in the time to process data subsets and gain knowledge and potential evidence from digital forensic data. The following chapters discuss the research undertaken in relation to applying and refining the observed time and data storage reductions observed in the pilot study to a wider range of data in investigation typologies, as well as examining the benefits in relation to analysis and data mining timeframes.

As highlighted in the pilot study, the indexing time for the full forensic copy was six hours, whereas the time to index the data subset was two minutes 53 s. In real-world cases, indexing can sometimes take more than 12 h, or many days to complete and with the size of data in some cases being so large (6 TB or larger is not uncommon), the index and database can become too large for typical software to function. Indexing has a valuable part to play in the forensic process, but the increasing time to index cases is becoming problematic and as such, indexing a data subset can provide improved time savings.

Reviewing the subset data for information that may have potential use in intelligence holdings is another benefit of the subset process as this can be undertaken quite rapidly. There is potential to utilise data mining or intelligence analysis software to streamline and automate intelligence analysis of the subset data. Chapter 4 examines in detail which files to collect as part of a data subset, as well as the process to collect standard files across a variety of cases, to ensure the greatest potential for data mining and intelligence analysis.

Cross-case analysis can provide a better understanding of criminal offending and networks, and potentially lead to disparate cases being linked and valuable intelligence gained.

An agency that seizes and analyses digital evidence should consider the reduction framework to rapidly triage and review media prior to full analysis to determine if relevant evidence is potentially located on the media. This can be used to prioritise full imaging of media according to the knowledge gained from the reduced dataset review. Forensic practitioners should consider storing subset data with backups of notes, reports and other common analysis files to answer questions that may arise subsequent to full analysis. DRbSI subset data can be stored in data holdings to enable research of historical case data and intelligence analysis, where legal authority exists.

The results of the pilot study were positive, and the ability to reduce data holdings to a smaller subset of data was better than anticipated. The next Chapter further explores the ability to reduce data volume to a subset data and undertake analysis in comparison with the full data, and compare the results to ensure the information being collected and stored in the subsets is appropriate to the task. Intelligence analysis techniques are reviewed in Volume 2, and appropriate techniques applied to the subset data and full forensic images to determine the benefits from undertaking this.

3.5   Summary

This chapter outlined the proposed Digital Forensic Data Reduction Framework, which serves to enlarge upon the process used for traditional forensic computer analysis with the initial steps of Commence (Scope) and Prepare. The steps for data reduction, data mining, and external source data are included and able to run concurrently with Preservation and Evidence Analysis. The framework allows a practitioner to move between subset analysis and full forensic analysis. This serves to expand common digital forensic analysis frameworks to be applicable when dealing with data subsets and intelligence analysis environments, including the addition of external source data, which may cause an investigation to branch in different directions.

This framework is used in the following chapters discussing the research of data reduction and data mining of digital forensic data holdings to (a) provide a guiding framework to step through a process of data reduction and analysis, as would be the case in digital forensic investigations, and (b) include a process of rapid analysis and intelligence analysis including external source data.

References

Abraham, T. (2006). Event sequence mining to develop profiles for computer forensic investigation purposes. In *ACSW Frontiers '06: Proceedings of the 2006 Australasian Workshops on Grid Computing and E-Research* (pp. 145–153).

ACPO. (2006). *Good practice guidelines for computer based evidence v4.0*, Association of Chief Police Officers viewed 5 March 2014, www.7safe.com/electronic_evidence.

Alink, W., Bhoedjang, R. A. F., Boncz, P. A., & de Vries, A. P. (2006). XIRAF–XML-based indexing and querying for digital forensics. *Digital Investigation, 3*(Suppl. 0), 50–58.

Alzaabi, M., Jones, A., & Martin, T. A. (2013). An ontology-based forensic analysis tool. *Journal of Digital Forensics, Security and Law, 2013*(Conference Supplement), 121–135.

Beebe, N. (2009). Digital forensic research: The good, the bad and the unaddressed. In *Advances in digital forensics* (pp. 17–36). Springer.

Beebe, N., & Clark, J. (2005). Dealing with terabyte data sets in digital investigations. In *Advances in digital forensics* (pp. 3–16).

Best_Buy. (2013). *WD–My Book Essential 3 TB External USB 3.0/2.0 Hard Drive–Black*, viewed 11 August 2013, http://www.bestbuy.com/site/WD—My-Book-Essential-3TB-External-USB-3.0/2.0-Hard-Drive—Black/1261281.p?id=1218244145647&skuId=1261281.

Bhoedjang, R. A. F., van Ballegooij, A. R., van Beek, H. M. A., van Schie, J. C., Dillema, F. W., van Baar, R. B., et al. (2012). Engineering an online computer forensic service. *Digital Investigation, 9*(2), 96–108.

Brown, R., Pham, B., & de Vel, O. (2005). Design of a digital forensics image mining system. In *Knowledge-based intelligent information and engineering systems* (pp. 395–404).

Bunting, S., & Wei, W. (2006). *EnCase computer forensics: The official EnCE: EnCaseCertified examiner study guide*. Indianapolis, IN: Wiley.

Carrier, B. (2005). *File system forensic analysis*. NJ: Addison-Wesley Boston.

Carvey, H. (2011). *Windows registry forensics: Advanced digital forensic analysis of the windows registry*. Elsevier.

Casey, E. (2011). *Digital evidence and computer crime: Forensic science, computers, and the internet*. Elsevier.

FBI_RCFL. (2003–2012). *FBI Regional Computer Forensic Laboratory Annual Reports 2003–2012*, FBI, Quantico.

Ferraro, M. M., & Russell, A. (2004). Current issues confronting well-established computer-assisted child exploitation and computer crime task forces. *Digital Investigation, 1*(1), 7–15.

Garfinkel, S. (2006a). Forensic feature extraction and cross-drive analysis. *Digital Investigation, 3,* 71–81.

Garfinkel, S. (2006b). Forensic feature extraction and cross-drive analysis. *Digital Investigation, 3* (Suppl. 0), 71–81.

Garfinkel, S. (2010) Digital forensics research: The next 10 years. *Digital Investigation, 7*(Suppl. 0), S64–S73.

Garfinkel, S., Farrell, P., Roussev, V., & Dinolt, G. (2009). *Bringing Science to Digital Forensics with Standardized Forensic Corpora, DFRWS 2009, Montreal, Canada*, DFRWS 2009, Montreal, Canada, viewed 9 September, http://digitalcorpora.org/corpora/disk-images.

Giri. (2012). *EMC Isilon 15 PB Storage system*, Giri Infrastructure, viewed 11 August, http://giriinfrastructure.blogspot.com.au/2012/01/emc-isilon-15pb-storage-system.html.

Greiner, L. (2009). Sniper forensics. *NetWorker, 13*(4), 8–10.

Hoelz, B., Ralha, C., & Geeverghese, R. (2009). Artificial intelligence applied to computer forensics. In *SAC '09: Proceedings of the 2009 ACM Symposium on Applied Computing* (pp. 883–888). ACM.

Huang, J., Yasinsac, A., & Hayes, P. J. (2010). Knowledge sharing and reuse in digital forensics. In *2010 fifth IEEE international workshop on systematic approaches to digital forensic engineering (SADFE)* (pp. 73–78) IEEE.

Justice, UDo. (2016). *Office of the Inspector General. Audit of the Federal Bureau of Investigation's New Jersey Regional Computer Forensic Laboratory*, https://oig.justice.gov/reports/2016/a1611.pdf.

Kenneally, E., & Brown, C. (2005). Risk sensitive digital evidence collection. *Digital Investigation, 2*(2), 101–119.

Lee, J., Un, S., & Hong, D. (2008). High-speed search using Tarari content processor in digital forensics. *Digital Investigation, 5,* S91–S95.

Marziale, L., Richard, G., & Roussev, V. (2007). Massive threading: Using GPUs to increase the performance of digital forensics tools. *Digital Investigation, 4,* 73–81.

McKemmish, R. (1999), *What is forensic computing?*

Nance, K., Hay, B., & Bishop, M. (2009) Digital forensics: Defining a research agenda. In *42nd Hawaii international conference on system sciences, 2009, HICSS'09* (pp. 1–6). IEEE.

NIJ. (2004). *Forensic examination of digital evidence: A guide for law enforcement*, http://nij.gov/nij/pubs-sum/199408.htm.

NIJ. (2008). *Electronic crime scene investigation: A guide for first responders* (2nd ed.), http://www.nij.gov/pubs-sum/219941.htm.

Palmer, G. (2001). A road map for digital forensic research. In *Report from the first digital forensic research workshop (DFRWS)*, August 7–8, 2001.

Parsonage, H. (2009). *Computer Forensics Case Assessment and Triage - some ideas for discussion*, viewed 4 August, http://computerforensics.parsonage.co.uk/triage/triage.htm.

Pollitt, M. M. (2013). Triage: A practical solution or admission of failure. *Digital Investigation, 10* (2), 87–88.

Pringle, N., & Sutherland, I. (2008). Is a computational grid a suitable platform for high performance digital forensics? In *Proceedings of the 7th European Conference on Information Warfare and Security* (p. 175). Academic Conferences Limited.

Quarnby, N., & Young, L. J. (2010). *Managing intelligence–The art of influence*. Sydney, Australia: The Federation Press.

Quick, D., & Choo, K. (2013a). Dropbox analysis: Data remnants on user machines. *Digital Investigation, 10*(1), 3–18.

Quick, D., & Choo, K. (2013b). Digital Droplets: Microsoft SkyDrive forensic data remnants. *Future Generation Computer Systems, 29*(6), 1378–1394.

Quick, D., & Choo, K.-K. R. (2013c). Forensic collection of cloud storage data: Does the act of collection result in changes to the data or its metadata? *Digital Investigation, 10*(3), 266–277.

Quick, D., & Choo, K.-K. R. (2014). Google drive: Forensic analysis of data remnants. *J. Network and Computer Applications, 40,* 179–193.

Quick, D., Martini, B., & Choo, K.-K. R. (2014). *Cloud storage forensics*. Syngress: An Imprint of Elsevier.

Raghavan, S. (2013). Digital forensic research: Current state of the art. *CSI Transactions on ICT, 1* (1), 91–114.

Raghavan, S., Clark, A., & Mohay, G. (2009). FIA: An open forensic integration architecture for composing digital evidence. In *Forensics in telecommunications, information and multimedia* (pp. 83–94). Springer.

Ratcliffe, J. (2003). Intelligence-led policing. *Trends and Issues in Crime and Criminal Justice, 248,* 1–6.

Reyes, A., Oshea, K., Steele, J., Hansen, J., Jean, B., & Ralph, T. (2007). *Digital forensics and analyzing data* (pp. 219–259). Cyber Crime Investigations: Elsevier.

Richard, G., & Roussev, V. (2006). Next-generation digital forensics. *Commun ACM, 49*(2), 76–80.

Roussev, V., & Richard, G. (2004). Breaking the performance wall: The case for distributed digital forensics. In *Proceedings of the 2004 Digital Forensics Research Workshop.*

Schatz, B., & Clark, A. J. (2006). An open architecture for digital evidence integration. In *AusCERT Asia Pacific information technology security conference, 21–26 May 2006.*

Shannon, M. (2004). Forensic relative strength scoring: ASCII and entropy scoring. *International Journal of Digital Evidence, 2*(4), 151–169.

Sheldon, A. (2005). The future of forensic computing. *Digital Investigation: The International Journal of Digital Forensics and Incident Response, 2*(1), 31–35.

Shiaeles, S., Chryssanthou, A., & Katos, V. (2013). On-scene triage open source forensic tool chests: Are they effective? *Digital Investigation, 10*(2), 99–115.

Suleman, K. (2011). *EMC World 2011: Isilon debuts 15 PB NAS single file storage system,* V3.co. uk, viewed 11 August, http://www.v3.co.uk/v3-uk/news/2069388/emc-world-2011-isilon-debuts-15pb-nas-single-file-storage.

Teelink, S., & Erbacher, R. (2006). Improving the computer forensic analysis process through visualization. *Communication of ACM, 49*(2), 71–75.

Turner, P. (2005). Unification of digital evidence from disparate sources (Digital Evidence Bags). *Digital Investigation, 2*(3), 223–228.

Turner, P. (2007). Applying a forensic approach to incident response, network investigation and system administration using Digital Evidence Bags. *Digital Investigation, 4*(1), 30–35.

UNODC. (2011). *United Nations office on drugs and crime–Criminal intelligence manual for analysts.* New York, Vienna, Austria: United Nations.

van Baar, R.B., van Beek, H. M. A., & van Eijk, E. J. (2014). Digital forensics as a service: A game changer. *Digital Investigation, 11*(Suppl. 1, no. 0), S54–S62.

Vidas, T., Kaplan, B., & Geiger, M. (2014). OpenLV: Empowering investigators and first-responders in the digital forensics process. *Digital Investigation, 11*(Suppl. 1, no. 0), S45–S53.

Chapter 4
Digital Forensic Data Reduction by Selective Imaging

In the previous chapters, the focus of the research was outlined, current literature was discussed, and the proposed Digital Forensic Data Reduction Framework was explained. This chapter focuses on Step 5 of the framework and explores the process of data reduction using the proposed framework to guide the research.

The application of a data reduction methodology to digital forensic data was discussed in the Literature Review. Beebe (2009), Beebe and Clark (2005) call for further research in relation to data reduction and data mining methods, and what should be collected. Due to differing legal requirements of diverse jurisdictions, a data reduction methodology may not necessarily replace full imaging and analysis in all cases, but serves to provide an alternative process to run alongside full analysis to rapidly triage, collect, review, and archive forensic data and support the various stages of digital forensic examinations. In instances such as terrorism and organised crime investigations, there is often a need to be able to rapidly process data.

4.1 Digital Forensic Data Reduction by Selective Imaging

The proposed digital forensic data reduction process using selective imaging (Fig. 4.1) outlined in this chapter is designed to provide for an overall reduction methodology for forensic data. However, it is not proposed to completely replace full forensic analysis. The reduction process is aimed to collect forensic subsets which contain potentially relevant data, and be able to store and search multiple subsets. A review of a data subset as opposed to a full forensic image may consequently speed up the forensic process by locating evidential data, or by providing examiners with a quick understanding of the data to enable a better focus for full

---

Material presented in this chapter is based on the following publication:

Quick, D. and K.-K. R. Choo, Big forensic data reduction: digital forensic images and electronic evidence. Cluster Computing, 2016. 19(2): p. 723–740.

analysis. It is recognised that there is a potential for evidential data residing in a large data source, such as unallocated space, to be missed in any reduction process, and there are instances where there has been a deliberate effort to hide data and information. Therefore the proposed reduction process is not aimed to be an replacement for full analysis, but is available as a process which can be run prior to or in conjunction with full imaging and analysis. If evidential data is not located during the subset collection, processing, and review, it is recommended to then undertake full imaging and analysis, as per current practices, and is listed in Fig. 4.1.

The proposed data reduction process is intended to collect files for further processing with other common digital forensic tools, such as Internet Evidence Finder, NUIX, Intella, EnCase, FTK, and other forensic tools. The process collects

Digital Forensic Data Reduction [HD or Storage Media]		
Commence	Outline focus and scope of investigation.	
Prepare	Ensure correct equipment and expertise.	
Identify and Collect	Identify devices with potential evidence/intelligence, photograph and document	
Write block / Load	1. Load forensic image, or mount write-blocked physical device.	
Process [optional]	Recover folders [optional – depending on time available] Signature analysis [optional – depending on time available] Hash calculation [optional – depending on time available]	
Select	2. Filter to display and select important files for data subset (specific files detailed in text) • File System • Operating System • Software, Internet History • User created; Emails, Documents, Pictures, Audio, Video	
Review	3. Review Pictures, select those that are relevant 4. Review other files, select those that are relevant	
	5. Deselect selected files which are marked as overwritten 6. Deselect large files (usually anything larger than the $MFT as a guide, but leave if important)	
Convert	[if necessary, mount forensic image as logical drive/s] 9. Convert Video files to thumbnail/s (e.g. using mtn batch file) 10. Shrink Picture files [1024 pixels wide/high] and place into Lo1	
Preserve	7. Export selected files to Lo1 or other forensic container 8. Export a File List to CSV and convert to XLSX or compress to ZIP	
Analysis of Subset	Conduct analysis of the subset for evidence and/or intelligence.	
Evidence located? Yes No	Full Image Analysis	If evidence or intelligence is not located, conduct analysis of full forensic image.
Presentation	Present the information in a report or verbal communication.	

Fig. 4.1 Digital forensic data reduction by selective imaging (DRbSI)—Step 5 of DFDR framework

a wide range of file and data types, including: documents, spreadsheets, pictures, videos, Internet browsing history, Internet chat, email, communications, Windows Registry files, Apple operating system files, iPhone backup folders, and many other file and data types, and is outlined in the next section.

The proposed Digital Forensic Data Reduction by Selective Imaging (DRbSI) is a process of collecting data with a focus on that which will potentially provide information relevant to an investigation in a rapid manner, with benefits in relation to volume and time savings. There are a large range of file and data types included in the collection process. Examples include, but are not limited to: Internet browser history files, Log files, Registry files, Word Documents, Spreadsheets, Email containers, and other Windows system files (as outlined in Table 4.1).

The data reduction method is intended to be undertaken alongside standard forensic processes, and hence there is still a need to retain the original evidence or media, as it may be necessary to access the original source data at a later stage. If the original media is only available for collection or preservation purposes (i.e. is not seized or retained), then a full forensic image should be undertaken. In instances where media has been seized or retained, there is an opportunity to initially focus on a subset of files prior to full imaging, which may result in alleviating the need for full imaging. With any reduction methodology there is a risk that evidence may not be in a subset of information. However, there is potentially less risk with this process in comparison with other methods designed to address data volume and timeliness concerns, such as forensic triage. A digital forensic triage process scans a selection of files and interprets the information, which limits the ability to undertake subsequent analysis with other tools. This method preserves original files and data in a forensic container, and provides for analysis of the forensic subset with a range of tools, not limited to one specific tool or process, and can be subsequently processed with triage or other software. A method of random sampling has also been raised in relation to data reduction and verification, however, as discussed in literature, utilising statistical or random data reduction methods will likely result in missing crucial evidence (Beebe 2009; Shannon 2004).

When undertaking any digital forensic process, compliance with digital forensic guidelines, such as those outlined in International Standard 27037 (ISO/IEC 2012), ACPO (2006), and NIJ (2004) is recommended. The reduction methodology can be applied to a forensic image (E01) file or write-blocked physical media. When working with physical media, write blocking is recommended, either using; software (Windows Registry key modification) and/or hardware (Tableau write blocking devices). Forensic software, such as EnCase or X-Ways, can be used to access a physical device, and "Conditions" or filters used to locate and select specific data and file types (outlined in Methods). The selected files are then preserved in a logical evidence container, such as: EnCase L01 or LX01, or X-Ways CTR format. There is also potential application of the method to cloud stored data, such as that within IaaS, where forensic preservation is one of the main issues, along with the sheer volume of data which potentially encourages the application of data reduction methodologies to enable analysis and gain an understanding of the data holdings (Alqahtany et al. 2015).

Table 4.1 Digital forensic data reduction filters/"conditions"

File System		
Category	Type	Data/Filename/File Extension
NTFS	Filename	INDX Buffer, $MFT, $Journal, $LogFile, $UsnJrnl
FAT	Filename	volumeboot, PrimaryFAT, SecondaryFAT, FAT1, FAT2, VBR
HFS/HFS+	Filename	DS_Store, journal, attributes, allocation, catalog, extents, MDB, +startup, volume header
EXT2/3/4	Filename	journal, superblock, inode table
Windows		
Registry	Filename	SAM, SYSTEM, SOFTWARE, SECURITY, NTUser.dat, UsrClass.dat
	Extension	.log, .reg (also consider restore point registry files)
Recycler &	Files	info2, $I, $R
Recycle Bin	Folder	\Recycler\ \Recycle.bin\
Logs	Filename	entries.log, ws-ftp.log
	Extension	.log, .wer, .log1, .log2, .log3, .log4...log9
Thumbnails	Filename	Thumbcache*.db, iconcache*.db, Thumbs.db, Thumbs.db.keep
	Extension	.keep (KEEP files can be opened with Thumb Expert)
	Folder	\Users\[user]\AppData\Local\Microsoft \Windows\Explorer\
Search Database	Filename	Windows.edb; MSS.chk, MSS.log, MSSTemp.log, tmp.edb, WSIndex
Config & Prefetch	Extension	.bak, .cfg, .pf
Link and Jumplist	Extension	.lnk, .fav
	Filename	*destinations (automatic and custom) – (Jumplist)
	Folder	\recent\
Event Logs	Extension	.evt, .evtx
Apple OSX		
plist files	Extension	.PLIST
	Filename	com.apple.finder.plist, addressbookme.plist
	Filename	com.apple.mail.plist, cookies.plist, com. apple.safari.plist
	Filename	com.apple.preview.bookmarks.plist, bookmarks.plist
	Filename	downloads.plist, history.plist, lastsession.plist
	Filename	com.apple.recentitems.plist
Database	Extension	.DB, apalbum
	Filetype	SQLite database files
Keychain	Filename	login.keychain

(continued)

File System		
Category	Type	Data/Filename/File Extension
User information	Filename	`addressbookme.data, addressbookme.data.previous`
Thumbnails	Extension	`.ithmb`
Calendar	Filename	`com.apple.ical`
Chat	Filename	`iChat.pictures`
Linux		
Files	Filename	`Strings`
	Filetype	`Bash History`
	Folder	Home (excluding Review Files, such as Picture and Videos)
Software and Applications		
Email	Extension	`msg, pst, dbx, eml, contact, imm`
	Folder	`\Thunderbird\`
	Filename	`showletter[1].htm, showfolder[1].htm`
Chat	Extension	`dat, ini, xml, xsl`
	Folder	`\myreceivedfiles\mychatlogs`
	Filename	`contacts.edb, wlcalenderstore.edbn, edb.chk, logs.cab`
	Folder	"windows messenger"
	Filename	`Xsslog`
	Filename	`journal, config`
	Filename	`hostname, cached-descriptors, cached-descriptors.new state`
	Filename	`cached-consensus`
Storage	Filename	`syncdiagnostic.log`
	Filename	`snapshot.db, sync_config.db`
	Filename	`config.db, filecache.db, config.dbx, filecache.dbx`
	Filename	`dropbox.cache, host.dbx, host.db, photo.dbx, sigstore.dbx`
	Extension	`Aol`
File sharing	Filename	`downloads.config; tracker.config`
	Filename	`AC_SearchStrings.dat, known.met`
	Folder	`\eMule`
	Extension	`BAK, DAT, INI, MET, OLD, TXT`
	Extension	`PROPS, CACHE, DAT`
	Filename	`fileurns.cache, downloads.dat, frostwire.props, library.dat`
	Filename	`createtimes.cache, application.xml, audio, limewire.props`
	Filename	`version.xml`

(continued)

File System		
Category	Type	Data/Filename/File Extension
		`Torrent`
Browsers		**[Mozilla Firefox]**
	Filename	`Places.sqlite.journal, CACHE_MAP,` `_CACHE_001_ 002_ 003_`
	Filename	`sessionstore`
	Folder	`\Mozilla\Firefox\Profiles\`
	Extension	`DB`
		[Opera Browser]
	Folder	`\Opera\"profile"\cache\, AppData\Roaming` `\Opera`
	Filename	`vlink4.dat, global_history.dat, bookmarks.` `adr, wand.dat`
	Filename	`cookies4.dat, Search_field.history.dat,` `Typed_history.xml`
	Filename	`Tasks.xml, Dcache4.url, bookmarks, resume.dat`
	Filename	`resume.dat.old, settings.dat, settings.dat.` `old,`
	Filename	`rss.dat, rss.dat.old, dht.dat, dht.dat.old,`
	Extension	`WIN (bookmarks)`
		[Google Chrome]
	Folder	`\Google\Chrome\UserData\`
	Filename	`cookies, currentsession, webdata,` `currenttabs, favicons`
	Filename	`journal, history, shortcuts, topsites, web` `data, data`
	Filetype	`Google Desktop Search`
		[Microsoft Internet Explorer]
	Folder	`\Temporary Internet Files\`
	Filename	`index.dat, webcache*.dat`
	Filetype	**`IE Recovery Store and Travel Log`**
	Extension	`JSON (bookmarks-2011-09-21.json)`
		[Apple Safari]
	Folder	`\AppleComputer\Safari\`
	Extension	`PLIST, DB (filenames are similar to Chrome filenames)`
	Filename	`TempPassword.$$$, syncdb, webbookmark,` `synciddb, webhistory`
Erasing	Filename	`eraser (and folder name "Eraser")`
	Extension	`ERS, TXT (Eraser)`
	Filename	`ccleaner (CCleaner)`
	Extension	`INI, TXT (and folder name "ccleaner", piriform)`

(continued)

File System		
Category	Type	Data/Filename/File Extension
Encryption	Filename	`bestcrypt` (and folder name "bestcrypt")
	Extension	`jbc` (bestcrypt extension)
	Filename	`truecrypt` (and folder name "truecrypt")
Media Player	Extension	`WMDB, WPL`
	Filename	`lastplayed.wpl`
Bitcoin, etc.	Folder	`Bitcoin, litecoin, dogecoin`
	Filename	`wallet.com` (db.log, debug.log)
Other	Filename	`README`
	Folder	`\AppleComputer\MobileSync\`
	Filename	`manifest.mbdb`
	Extension	`Ithmb`
	Extension	`NFO, INF, IPD`
User Files		
Documents	Extension	`doc, docx, dot, wri, rtf, odt, odg, ods, ots, pdf`
	Extension	`xls, xlsx, xlsm, ppt, pptx, myob`
Pictures	Extension	`jpg, bmp, png, gif, psd, jpeg, tif, tiff` (Collect or reduce)
Videos	Extension	`wmv, avi, mov, mpg, mp4, flv, 3gp, mts, vob` (Collect or thumbnail)
Audio	Extension	`mp3, wav, amr, ogg, m4a, wma` (Review)
Review		
Pictures	Extension	`bmp, jpg, png, gif, tif, tiff, psd`
Videos	Extension	`wmv, avi, mov, mpg, mp4, m2v, flv, 3gp, mts, vob`
Audio	Extension	`mp3, wav, amr, ogg, m4a, wma`
Containers	Extension	`iso, zip, rar, wim, dd, 001 ... 009`
	Extension	`vmdk, vmem, vmx`
	Extension	`Jbc`
Other	Extension	`db3, edb, htm, html` (review htm files or convert to text for index)
Exclude /Review		
Other	Extension	`ttf, wmf, qtr, sys, dll, exe, cab, fon, gpd, hlp, msi`
	Extension	`man, manifest, mum, mui, pnf, ppd, jdk, jre, ico, ipa`
	Filename	`HCdata.edb, licence.rtf, datastore.edb`

4.1.1 Load or Mount Forensic Image or Connect Physical Device

Once potential evidential media is identified, the next step of the process involves enabling forensic access to the source media, either the physical device or a full forensic image. When the data reduction methodology is undertaken, recommended forensic best practice should be adhered to. Even if not undertaken as part of a forensic investigation, i.e. for a breach of policy investigation or intelligence purposes, it is recommended to utilise common forensic practices, as it is possible that evidence of a crime may become apparent, in which case recommended forensic practices would be necessary. Therefore, physical media or devices should be attached utilising hardware or software write blocking to ensure no data is altered where possible (as per ACPO (2006); ISO/IEC (2012) or NIJ (2004)). Forensic compliance is not an onerous undertaking, and serves to prevent issues which may arise later in the scope of an investigation.

4.1.2 Processing Options

Using forensic software (such as EnCase Forensic or X-Ways Forensic), there are processes which can be undertaken prior to data reduction filters being run. This includes processing, such as: the EnCase 'Recover Folders' process which is a scan of the drive for file table remnants. However, these processes can be potentially time consuming. Although they may result in additional files being identified, risk management considerations needs to be made by the practitioner in relation to undertaking various pre-processing, weighing up the potential to recover data, in balance with the time to undertake the process.

A method of anti-forensics where file contents are obfuscated by altering file extensions can result in a filtering process missing key files. A process of File Signature Analysis, whereby each file is examined to compare the file extension in relation to the header to identify the actual data in a file, is able to locate altered files. This can identify files with an incorrect extension, and files with a known underlying format, such as a SQL database with a .dat or other extension. This process can be run to locate files with differing or incorrect extensions, but again needs to be balanced with the time to undertake this process.

Hash analysis is another pre-process, and consists of calculating a hash value using MD5 and/or SHA algorithms to calculate a unique value for each file. This process can be important, but can also be time consuming. A forensic practitioner can balance the importance of the hash value in comparison with the time to undertake this.

If on-site, time considerations may preclude undertaking these pre-processes, but in a lab situation there may be time available to undertake these or other pre-processes to refine or discover new data. Whilst it is possible to calculate hash values for the files selected and preserved subsequent to the reduction process, any files not included cannot subsequently have a hash value calculated, as the contents are not included in a logical (L01) file. The forensic practitioner needs to weigh up the need for undertaking these processes with the time available (listed in the Process section of Fig. 4.1).

4.1.3 Filters for Subset Files

Once any pre-processing is complete, filters are then applied to identify files and data for imaging (the "Identify" step in Fig. 4.1). The decision to include or exclude particular file types is based on an understanding of the contents and value of the information contained within common file types. This section outlines the various files and typologies of potentially relevant information, and is discussed in sections broken down into: File System, Operating System, Software and Applications, and User Created Data (listed in Table 4.1).

4.1.4 File System Filters

File systems have various data files which contain potentially relevant information, and hence are important for collection. As an example, the NTFS file system has files of interest which include: $MFT, $Journal, $LogFile, and $UsnJrnl (listed in Table 4.1). The FAT file system has: volumeboot, PrimaryFAT, SecondaryFAT, FAT1, FAT2, and VBR. The Apple File Systems HFS and HFS+ have various files, such as: journal, attributes, catalog, and MDB. There are a variety of file systems in use with Linux operating systems, such as EXT3, EXT4, and others, which have common files of interest, such as: journal, superblock, and inode table. These files can contain potentially relevant data, and therefore are included in the filters. In Table 4.1, the type of file and/or locations of interest are listed, such as: filename, file extension, or folder location. In the Data section, the filenames, file extension, or folder location is listed to enable practitioners to build conditions or filters to be used in forensic software to view and select these specific files or locations.

4.1.5 Operating System Filters

There are many files of potential forensic interest contained within Operating Systems. This section of Table 4.1 focuses on files of interest observed in Microsoft Windows, Apple OSX, and Linux installations. Files located within Windows operating systems for inclusion in a data reduction filter include files such as: Registry files, Recycler, Log Files, Thumbnails, Config files, Prefetch, and Link

Files. Files of interest located within the Apple OSX operating system are listed in Table 4.1. Unlike Windows, files in Apple operating systems may not necessarily have a file extension, so there may be a need to run a File Signature Analysis prior to using a data subset filter. In addition, filters should include filename, file type, and file extension values. Whilst there are many variations of the Linux operating system, there are some generic files that are common to many distributions, also outlined in Table 4.1.

4.1.6 Software and Applications Filters

There are many software and applications with files of potential relevance. Table 4.1 outlines the types of files targeted in the reduction process for collection. The table is divided into sections with a focus on differing file types, including Email, Chat, Storage, File sharing, Internet Browsers, and other file types. Email, Chat, and other communication type files are of potential importance as these can often store information which may be relevant to an investigation.

4.1.7 User Data Filters

User Data type files are listed in Table 4.1 and consist of files such as documents and spreadsheets, pictures and video, and audio. These are files usually created by a user, and not necessarily created by the operating system, software or application internal file. Whilst an entire User folder can be included in a data reduction collection process, care should be taken to ensure unnecessary files are not included, and files of large size are reviewed. As previously mentioned, the decision when to collect all files or a subset of files would be a consideration of a forensic practitioner relating to timeliness constraints and the scope of a request, these risk management considerations needs to be made by the practitioner with an understanding of the needs of analysis in relation to undertaking various processes. It is difficult to list specific occasions when data reduction is applicable versus full analysis, as this needs to take into account the scope of a request, i.e. there are some homicide investigations where analysis of a data subset is appropriate, and other cases where full analysis is necessary. Likewise, some drug cases benefit from rapid analysis of a subset, and others require full analysis, depending on the scope of the enquiry. Files such as video and movies can be thumbnailed or reviewed as these can take up a large amount of space, especially video files (which could be thumbnailed as discussed in the Video Thumbnail section).

4.1.8   Review of Large Files

Some files are large and may contain valuable information, such as ZIP files, ISO files, and other large container type files. These files can be reviewed to determine whether to be included in a subset. The file types for review are listed in Table 4.1. If a practitioner locates the presence of Virtual Computer type containers (such as VMDK) it is possible to load the VMDK file into the forensic software, and run data reduction filters across the VMDK internal files to collect relevant files from within the VMDK, rather than collecting the entire VMDK file which can be quite large.

4.1.9   Excluded File Types and Overwritten Files and Data

There are file types which can be excluded when not of potential need of an investigation, such as executable files and dll files. Typical files which can be excluded are listed in Table 4.1. The type of files which are not collected in the examples listed in Table 4.1 include executable (exe) files, dynamic link library (dll) files, font (fon) files, help (hlp) files, icon (ico) files, manual (man) files, and other file types. However, for cyber-crime type offences (for example; modification of executables) these can be included or reviewed, or undertake hash analysis to exclude known files. In addition, files which are marked as overwritten are not collected, as the data contained at the location has been overwritten with other data and as such does not necessarily represent a file of interest.

The files not collected are those which are unlikely to contain evidence applicable to a user or user action, such as dll files which are used by software. If a case relates to modification of executables or dll files, then these file types should be collected. If it is suspected there may be evidence in a file type, such as a cab file, these should be collected in the subset for analysis.

4.1.10   File and Data List (Spreadsheet) Report

A list of all files and data on media is then created, in a spreadsheet format. This serves to preserve the metadata information about all files, such as: creation dates, modification times, sector locations, logical size, etc. As an example, using EnCase Forensic software, the "*Export*" function in EnCase 6, or the "*Save As*" function in EnCase 7, a comma separated value file is created with all file and data entries listed with associated metadata.

4.1.11   Video Thumbnails Method

Video files are often quite large, and rarely compress further as many formats are already compressed. Hence, these files can consume a large amount of digital forensic image volume. An alternative method proposed is take thumbnail images of video frames at certain intervals, and store the thumbnail picture rather than the full video file. Using software such as "mtn—movie thumbnailer", or "ThumbnailMe", a directory structure can be traversed, and video files can be processed to output thumbnail pictures at regular intervals. An example of output from this type of process is displayed in Fig. 4.2, which shows a thumbnailed video file which was originally a 750 MB mp4 video file, and resulted in a 176 KB jpg file. Referring to the picture it is easy to determine the contents of the video file without playing or storing the entire video.

An additional benefit, the thumbnail process can assist when explaining the contents of video to Investigators, Prosecutors, and Court, by providing thumbnail files. This may potentially alleviate the need to organise facilities to play video to various persons involved in the investigation or prosecution. This is also beneficial when providing evidence to court, as the need to copy every selected video file to a disc can be time consuming and require large amounts of storage, whereas the thumbnails can be easily included on CD or DVD media, or printed out. Using software such as Movie Thumbnailer (mtn) (http://moviethumbnail.sourceforge.net/) or ThumbnailMe3 software (http://www.thumbnailme.com/) the process of thumb-nailing can be quite fast, and result in dramatic reductions in storage requirements (See Discussion for examples). When a review is undertaken of the video thumbnails,

Fig. 4.2 Example of video thumbnail from software ThumbnailMe

relevant files can be determined, and the full video collected from the original media if required for evidence or further analysis of the contents. The process of thumbnailing video can also be enhanced with the application of semantic linked network analysis and representation to give context to video files where possible (Hu et al. 2014; 2015; Xu et al. 2014d; 2015).

4.1.12 Picture Dimension Reduction

Whilst picture files are relatively small, there can often be many thousands or millions on electronic media and storage seized for analysis. Collecting all pictures within a logical container is possible, and doesn't usually result in subsets that are too large. However, some cases may have enormous volumes of pictures. A similar process to thumbnailing video files can be implemented in these situations, by reducing the dimensions of picture files, as an example to 800×600 pixels, and converting all pictures to jpg files. Using software, such as XnView or ImageMagick, to batch process and scan mounted images or physical devices, dimension reduced pictures can be saved for review or intelligence purposes. By using this process, the storage and processing times for picture files can be reduced, potentially enabling the application of a variety of analysis methods, such as; inferring emotions from facial elements (Alhussein 2016).

Reducing the size of pictures to 1024 or 800 pixels wide will result in smaller size pictures in which details can still be discerned, such as written text for optical character recognition. In cases with very large volume of pictures, it may be more appropriate to have an examiner review pictures in a gallery view, and select relevant pictures. The method outlined in (Jones et al. 2012) outlines a method to collect a random selection of pictures. However, random selection may result in missing crucial evidence (Beebe 2009; Shannon 2004). In cases with very large volumes of picture files, it would also be possible to create thumbnail contact sheets or reduce or the size of the pictures to smaller dimensions.

4.1.13 Preservation

Once the filtered files have been selected, and any video thumbnails and/or picture files are loaded into the forensic software as 'single files', the logical image (L01) file/s can be created. The next section outlines the results of data reduction on test files, using the methods described and EnCase conditions based on Fig. 4.1.

4.2 Test Data Application and Results

To outline the application of the proposed Digital Forensic Data Reduction by Selective Imaging (DRbSI) process, the M57 image file "*2008-m57-jean.E01*" from Digital Forensic Corpus (Garfinkel et al. 2009b) is used as an example. This is a forensically imaged hard drive with a Windows Operating System. The original Physical hard drive was **10 GB**, and the full forensic image file was in the **E01** format, and totalled **2.83 GB**. It is acknowledged that this M57 file is a sparse file designed for training purposes, and is used here as an example to outline the process rather than determine the efficiency of the process. The efficiency of the process is discussed when applied to a range of test cases (Table 4.3) and real world case files (Table 4.4). The filters used are those outlined in Table 4.1.

The M57 E01 image file was loaded into EnCase 6.19.7, and EnCase Conditions (Table 4.1) were used to filter and display the files for inclusion in a reduced subset, comprising: Operating System Files, Documents, Email, and Internet files. This process can also be undertaken in EnCase 7, which was also tested for this research, with similar times and results observed.

The filtered files displayed in EnCase 6 were selected, and comprised **7,676 files** totalling **470.2 MB.** In addition, the picture file filter condition was run, and **5,442 pictures** were selected, comprising a total of **18.1 MB**. The selected files were then reviewed for large files, and overwritten files were removed. The selected files were then saved to a Logical Forensic container (L01) file which resulted in a **183 MB L01** logical image file (**1.83% of the original hard drive**). The creation of the logical image file took **26 s**.

A list of all files and metadata was created using the EnCase "Export" function to export a list of information in "CSV" format. This was then opened and saved in Microsoft Excel "XLSX" format, resulting in a **6.03 MB** file.

To determine the information value within the Digital Forensic Data Reduction DRbSI L01 files, a comparison was then run by processing with EnCase 7.09.03. The same processing options were used for both the E01 and L01 images, consisting of: Signature Analysis, Hash value calculation, all Email types, and comprehensive Internet History. The time for EnCase to verify the **E01 file** was **1 min 25 s,** and **3 min 1 s to process, totalling 4 min 26 s**. In comparison, the **L01** took **3 s to verify,** and **30 s to process, totalling 33 s**.

The types of files discovered are listed in Table 4.2. Whilst the L01 represents only **1.83%** of the volume of the original hard drive: **all** emails, documents, spreadsheets, and pictures, and the majority of the Internet History entries; **98.02%,** were present in the subset. The E01 Internet history entries were compared with the L01 Internet history entries, the difference in the results related to overwritten duplicate entries in the E01, the data for the original entry was located in the L01 and the information was not absent. The M57 image file "2008-m57-jean.E01" was prepared as an academic study for students, and the evidence in this case file consists of certain files and types, which were collected in the subset.

As this example is a relatively small hard disk drive (10 GB), processing times for larger drives show much larger differences in processing a full forensic image (E01) in comparison with a subset of files (L01). As an example, the Corpus "*nps-2011-scenario4.E01*" was originally a 250 GB drive, the processing options in EnCase 7.09.03 (as above) were used, and resulted in the E01 taking 27m10 s to verify, and 8 m 12 s to process, a **total of 35 m 22 s**. The data reduction L01 file took 14 s to verify, and 37 s to process, a **total of 51 s**. After processing, **99.8% of the user files** were in the case file, and **44.23% of the Internet history** information, from an **L01 which is 0.23%** of the volume of the drive, and only **2.4% of the time** to process.

The methodology outlined for the test case was applied to a selection of cases from the Digital Corpora and the M57 case sets (Garfinkel et al. 2009b). Initial experiments determined there was a reduction to **0.75%** of the original hard drive size for the subset files from the M57 and Corpora forensic images (see the Pilot Study in the previous Chapter). This research has further expanded on the number of file types being collected, resulting in a median average of **1.08% L01:HD**, and when all original size picture files were included resulted in **1.27%** of the original source media. There was an average file size of 365 MB per L01 file, and an average of 34 s to create each L01 (Table 4.3).

4.3 Application to Real World Digital Forensic Case Data

The Digital Forensic Data Reduction by Selective Imaging method was applied to a selection of real world cases of an Australia Law Enforcement Agency; South Australia Police (SAPOL) Electronic Crime Section (ECS). The contents of the case files were not viewed, with only the metadata relating to the data volume and processing times collated.

4.3.1 Real World Data Subset Reduction

The proposed data reduction methodology outlined was applied to a selection of cases (different to the original experiments in the Pilot Study), resulting in a median reduction to **0.206%** of the source volume in **3.78% of the time** (Table 4.4). In the pilot study, the average reduction of data was reduced to **0.196%** of the total evidence volume (Chap. 3). The difference can be attributed to different source files, and additional files being included in the data reduction methodology to the initial experiments, resulting in larger L01 files, but includes additional information.

As in the experiments in the Pilot Study, the figures of the M57 and Corpus files differ to the reduction percentages observed with the South Australia Police Electronic Crime Section files as the M57 and Corpus image files appear to be

Table 4.2 Comparison of processing M57 file "2008-m57-jean" E01 and L01 in EnCase 7.09.03

	Files	Mismatches	Hast values	Internet History entries	Email messages	Documents	Spread Sheets	Pictures	Total
E01	32792	1241	32767	12727	309	311	15	5440	18802
L01	10925	124	9950	12475	309	311	15	5440	18550
Percentage L01: E01	33,32%	9.99%	30.37%	98.02%	100%	100%	100%	100%	98.66%

based on smaller hard disk drives with purpose built scenarios rather than the larger hard drives observed in the Electronic Crime Section files.

4.3.2 Real World Data—Video Thumbnailing

The process of thumbnailing video files was also applied to a sample of real world cases with significant data reduction percentages observed. As an example of the storage size reduction; a **500 GB** hard drive containing 828 video files totalling **399.3 GB**, which when all video files were thumbnailed reduced to **134 MB** of snapshot files for the 828 files (in the format of Fig. 4.2), reflective of **0.034%** of the original video volume. Another example comprised a **500 GB** hard drive storing **279 GB** of video files, which reduced to **118 MB** of video thumbnails, or **0.042%** of the video files.

To compare the times for capturing the video thumbnails to collecting a full forensic image (E01) file; for a case with a 1 TB hard drive and a 500 GB hard drive took 23 h and 15 min to acquire a full image, resulting in E01 files of 861 GB and 454 GB respectively. In comparison, using the Data Reduction by Selective Imaging method across the hard drives to collect a subset of data as described resulted in 1.3 GB and 78 MB L01 files in 3 min and 13 s. The video thumbnails took 1 h and 52 min to collect thumbnail snapshots of all video files, resulting in 217 MB and 118 MB. The total volume of E01 files comprised 1.3 TB, and the Data Reduction L01 files and Video Thumbnails comprised 1.713 GB, reducing to 0.11% of the original data volume. It was noted that the additional time to process the video files for hard drive one appeared to be due to network issues at the time of testing, with an observed median time to thumbnail video files from a range of hard drives over a larger period of time was 18 min on average.

In practice, investigating officers were able to review thumbnail video files at a far greater speed than when reviewing the original video files, and due to the method of being able to view up to 25 snapshots from each video in one image, were able to locate potential evidential video items from amongst many thousands of video files in a rapid manner.

4.3.3 Real World Data—Case Examples and Post Case Analysis

The Digital Forensic Data Reduction process has been applied to a range of real world cases comprising over one hundred terabytes of storage media. In some cases these would previously have taken up to a fortnight to fully forensically image and process before being ready for an investigator to review. In one example, a case comprised of multiple computers and storage devices, totalling 8.57 TB.

Table 4.3 Selective Imaging applied to M57 (Garfinkel 2009) case files

	HD (GB)	E01 (GB)	LDl (MB)	L01 time (s)	L01: E01 (%)	L01: HD
2008 m57 Jean	10	2.83	183	26	6.47	1.83
4Dell Latitude	4.5	1	50.1	8	5.01	1.11
charlic-2009-11-12	9.5	3.02	142	22	4.70	1.49
charlic-2009-12-11	9.5	3.6	402	43	11.17	4.23
jo-2009-11-12	12.1	3.06	165	20	5.39	1.36
jo-2009-11-20 old	12.1	3.72	464	43	12.47	3.83
jo-2009-11-20 new	14.3	2.19	98.8	12	4.51	0.69
jo-2009-12-11-002	14.3	5.53	547	57	9.39	3.83
pat -2009-11-12 start	12.1	2.98	127	16	4.26	1.05
pat-2009-12-11	12.1	5.72	54 S	60	9.56	4.53
Terry-2009-12-11-001	38.3	9.84	604	44	6.14	1.58
tracy-external-2012-07-03- initial	13.2	3.47	0.523	1	0.02	0.004
tracy-external-2012-07-16-final	13.2	3.5	0.989	1	0.03	0.01
tracy-external-2O12-07-03-initial VDMK	12	3.79	392	37	10.34	3.27
tracy-external-2012-07-16-final VMDK	12	3.81	348	32	9.13	2.90
tracy-home-2012-07-03 –initial	17.4	5.29	1110	77	20.98	6.38
tracy-home-2012-07-16-final	17.4	5.39	1130	73	20.96	6.49
nps-2009-domexusers	40	4.07	175	21	4.30	0.44
nps-2011-scenario 1	74.5	34.5	382	44	1.11	0.51
nps-201 l-scenario 4	2328	18.1	526	49	2.91	0.23
Total	381.3 GB		7.4 GB	34 s average		1.27

Estimations indicated it would take approximately a week of imaging and a week of processing to have ready for an investigator to review. By using the Digital Forensic Data Reduction by Selective Imaging (DRbSI) process to collect a subset of relevant files, and thumbnailing the video files, the volume of data collected was reduced to 12.3 GB, in under 2 h. The data subsets were processed in NUIX in 23 min, and available for the investigator to review. The subsets were reviewed by the Investigating Detective, and crucial evidential files including pictures and videos were selected, exported, and reports produced. In many cases this time difference of hours compared to weeks, can be crucial to rapidly progress an investigation with persons or children at risk.

Post case analysis was undertaken to review the potential risk of relevant evidence not being included in the data reduction L01 files. A comparison was undertaken after an Investigator or Detective had conducted a review of files and information contained within the full forensic image (E01) of electronic media. A random selection of cases were made, and E01 files were loaded into EnCase

Table 4.4 SAPOL ECS digital forensic data reduction results

Image	HD (GB)	E01 (GB)	E01 time	L01 (GB)	L01 Time	E01:HD (%)	L01:HD (%)
LTHD	500	47.9	3 h 30 min	1.03	3 min 45 s	9.58	0.21
MAC HD	1000	260	17 h 00 min	3.16	14 min 07 s	26.00	0.32
PCHD	1000	47.3	2 h 49 min	1.08	6 min 26 s	4.73	0.11
LTHD	120	87	1 h 5 min	0.74	5 min 37 s	72.50	0.62
PCHD	150	100	50 min	141	5 min 09S	66.67	0.94
PCHD	160	119	1 h 4 min	I.06	2 min 25 s	74.38	0.66
PCHD	1000			0.633	1 min 02 s		0.06
PCHD	1000			0.557	1 min 00 s		0.04
PCHD	2000			0.776	12 min 40 s		0.18
PCHD	320			0.578	2 min 25 s		
MACLTHD	500	49.2	3 h 12 min	1.38	9 min 03 s	9.84	0.28
PCHD	500	160	3 h 03 min	2.11	12 s	32.00	0.42
PCHD	500	22.7	6 h 47 min	0.0598	7 min 56 s	4.54	0.01
LTHD	60	34.4	39 min	1.68	5 min 41 s	57.-33	2.80
LTHD	120	81	1 h 05 min	1.46	14 s	67.50	1.22
HD	500	454	4 h 00 min	0.0782	36 s	90.80	0.02
HD	320	218	2 h 46 min	0.327	2 min 07 s	63.13	0.10
VSEHD	1000	861	19 h 15 min	1.399	2 min 59 s	86.10	0.14
PCHD	40	29,6	20 min	1.17	36 s	74.00	0.23
USB HD	750	588	11 h 08 min	0.268	40 s	78.40	0.04
USBHD	1500	1180	23 h 35 min	0.0399	13 s	78.67	0.00
LTHD	80	12.6	34 min	1.17	3 min 33 s	15.75	1.46
PCHD	500	170	2 h 57 min	2.36	20 min 34 s	34.00	0.47
Total	**9300**	**4522**		**23–4**		**48.6**	**0.172**

6.19.7 and the Data Reduction by Selective Imaging filters and process applied to produce data subsets in L01 containers. The review process consists of an Investigator using NUIX software to examine the data contained within E01 files, and use tags to select files and data of relevance to a case. Reports are created using NUIX pertaining to the files selected to include the file name, path, creation and other data and times, and other information reported. These NUIX reports were reviewed to compare the filenames of the selected evidential files to the corresponding Digital Forensic Data Reduction subset L01 containers. In twelve (12) cases examined, **all** of the files selected as being of evidential value by the Detective or Investigating Officer were present in the data subset. This reinforces the hypothesis that an Investigator can conduct a review of a subset of data and locate potential evidential information, and the validity of the process. The cases involved were real world cases involving a range of evidential files selected by experienced investigators.

4.3.4 Real World Data—Cross Case Analysis

To explore the potential for cross-case analysis, a review was also undertaken across 472 L01 subset files comprising 303 GB of data by loading the forensic subset L01 files into EnCase 6.19.7. This was undertaken to determine a hypothetical case of which of the media and devices may contain Skype data holdings. From the subsets it was possible to determine that 116 of the data subsets held Skype 'main.db' files and other Skype database files, out of 8,127,735 total file and data entries. Attempting to load 472 full forensic images (E01) into EnCase would potentially be unfeasible, and take a considerable amount of time to navigate and search, and require considerable storage volume to host the image files. This process of storing and being able to rapidly process and search a reduced subset of relevant data enables the application of a digital forensic intelligence capability, such as that outlined by Ribaux et al. (2010) as the third role of forensic scientists, that of forensic intelligence. The potential for cross case analysis is further explored in Volume 2.

4.3.5 Real World Data—Failing Hard Disk Drives

In a SAPOL ECS case in January 2015, a hard disk drive seized for analysis was unable to be imaged as it had errors in multiple sectors causing the forensic software to crash within the first stages of imaging, and the resulting corrupted E01 image files were unable to be opened. The DRbSI method was used by the officer to collect a subset of files from the failing drive, which completed without error. This enabled the collection of files and the investigator was able to conduct a review of the collected files, which otherwise would not have been possible as the full image was unable to be completed (Personal Communication 30 January, 2015).

4.4 Discussion

Ongoing improvements in technology development in recent years, coupled with growing volume of data, has led to backlogs of digital forensic work and increasing times for imaging and processing. The digital forensic data reduction method outlined in this chapter has highlighted an opportunity to reduce the volume of data for imaging and processing by honing in on data of potential relevance without significant human interaction. The process outlined can be applied to either physical media or forensic images to reduce imaging and/or processing times. This can be utilised for a range of purposes, including: triage, review, analysis, archive, cross-case analysis, and intelligence analysis.

In the previous section the process was applied to test data, and applied to real world data. As was highlighted in these sections, there are considerable gains to be made in reducing the time to collect data, and the time to process data. Another benefit is that the collected source data can also be processed in a range of forensic tools, for example, processing a subset L01 image file using Magnet Forensics Internet Evidence Finder (IEF). To compare the information within an L01 to a full forensic image, IEF v6.4.1.0035 was used to process each E01 forensic image with a Full search and a Quick search, and then the L01 was processed. Using the 2008-m57-jean.E01 file, a full search took 15 min and 18 s to locate 45,060 entries. An IEF 'quick search' of the forensic image took 2 min and 19 s to locate 30,620 entries. In comparison, the processing time of the L01 was 2 min 1 s, locating 30,823 entries.

The data reduction figures and times observed have demonstrated the potential to reduce the times and volume in comparison with undertaking full forensic imaging, although it should be noted that this process does not replace full analysis, and there will be many instances where full imaging, processing, and analysis is necessary. The Digital Forensic Data Reduction method outlined has been observed in real world circumstances to enable faster imaging and processing, providing investigators access to data in a timely manner to progress investigations at a faster rate. The process can potentially provide timely results for a range of investigation types, such as: child exploitation, terrorism, organised crime, fraud, homicide, and for internal inquiries, such as employee misuse or intellectual property theft.

By reducing the volume of data holdings to enable faster processing, there are opportunities to apply a variety of intelligence and analysis methodologies to the forensic data holdings, such as extracting semantic links to build association link networks and document context and clustering (Luo et al. 2011; Xu et al. 2014a, b), using fuzzy comprehensive evaluation methods (Wei et al. 2015), building semantic relationships between entities (Xu et al. 2014c) and keyword association linked networks (Xuan et al. 2015). Geographical data can potentially be extracted from the data subsets for further processing such as by using the methods outlined in (Zhao et al. 2015). There is also an opportunity to use a data reduction approach to triage data holdings in relation to insider threat cases, and enable a faster process of analysis to discount suspected sources which may later turn out to be innocent (Punithavathani et al. 2015). The reduction process can also be used to triage suspected sources of network attacks identified using network traffic analysis, such as that in Ghaleb (2015).

There has been an ongoing growth in data presented for digital forensic analysis, which combined with the predicted growth in storage and devices is estimated to continue to grow in the coming years, further contributing to large backlogs of evidence awaiting analysis. The application of a data reduction process is one way to improve the time to image, process, and examine media. The proposed Digital Forensic Data Reduction process outlined in this chapter serves to greatly reduce the time and storage demands of forensic examinations. In addition, this potentially addresses a range of issues, including; forensic triage, analysis, intelligence analysis, presentation, storage, cold case future review, and archive. Data reduction can also lead to a better understanding of the information contained within forensic data holdings at a reduced storage cost, which will lead to a significant productivity gain for law enforcement and government agencies and in turn society.

The Digital Forensic Data Reduction process can be utilised as a triage method to gain a rapid understanding of data to assess which media or devices may contain potential evidence, and should be examined as a priority. The data reduction process may also alleviate the need for full analysis if the required information is discovered upon first review of a subset. Should evidential information not be located during a review of a subset of data, full analysis should be undertaken across a full forensic image. Observed were time reductions to a median of 14 min to collect a logical image and process in Internet Evidence Finder, as opposed to the median time of 8 h 4 min to process a full forensic image. The Data Subset L01 image files can also be utilised for cross-device and cross-case analysis, which may lead to links being discovered between disparate devices and cases. This further serves to add to the benefits of the data reduction by selective imaging process, and enables an ability to provide a digital forensic intelligence capability.

This research has applied a data reduction process to a range of test and real-world media to determine the information value of the subset in comparison with a full image. Volume 2 explores applying the methodology to mobile devices, and applying intelligence analysis methodologies to the data subsets. Law enforcement and government agencies that seize and analyse digital evidence should consider a data reduction methodology, such as the one outlined in this chapter, as another tool in the digital forensic tool-chest for triage and review of media, to quickly determine information holdings, and archive relevant information for future enquiries. In addition, the process outlined can be applied with common digital forensic hardware and software solutions available in appropriately equipped forensic labs without requiring additional purchase of software or hardware.

When applied to test cases, a hundredfold reduction of original media volume was observed. When applied to real world cases of an Australian Law Enforcement Agency, the data volume further reduced to a small percentage of the original media volume whilst retaining key evidential files and data. The reduction process was applied to a range of real world cases reviewed by experienced investigators and detectives and highlighted that evidential data was present in the data reduced forensic subset files. The process can be applied to a wide variety of cases, such as terrorism and organised crime investigations, and the proposed data reduction process is intended to provide a capability to rapidly process data and gain an understanding of the information and/or locate key evidence or intelligence in a timely manner.

The outcomes of this research proved to be beneficial in a number of real world Police investigations when hard drives were unable to be imaged or processed. The DRbSI process was used to collect a subset of data, when the full forensic image collection process continually failed, or the processing of a full forensic image failed. The details of the investigations cannot be expanded as they are ongoing, but it is important to highlight the real-world application of this research, including the use of the process in situations not initially envisioned, i.e. data collection when a drive is failing or data volume is too large to process with current software and tools. This demonstrates the research is already achieving the goals of enabling analysis of increasingly larger volumes of data, and enabling analysis when current collection methods fail.

4.5   Summary

This chapter outlined the proposed Digital Forensic Data Reduction by Selective Imaging (DRbSI) process, and included a detailed description of the proposed method to collect a subset of data. The process of data reduction is outlined and is able to run concurrently with preservation and analysis of full forensic images. The process allows a practitioner to collect a subset of data without compromising the ability to undertake full forensic imaging or full forensic analysis.

This data subsets resulting from the DRbSI process are utilised in Volume 2. As mentioned, this process enables forensic examiners to collect a subset of data, and is directly applicable to real-world investigations, and also serves to be applicable for research purposes.

In Volume 2, the Quick Analysis process is outlined, which addresses Step 6 and Step 8 of the framework. The process is outlined and experiments undertaken using the DRbSI data subsets and the test data corpus and again applying this to real world data to demonstrate the application of the findings.

References

ACPO. (2006). *Good practice guidelines for computer based evidence v4.0*, Association of Chief Police Officers viewed 5 March 2014, www.7safe.com/electronic_evidence.

Alhussein, M. (2016). Automatic facial emotion recognition using weber local descriptor for e-Healthcare system. *Cluster Computing*, 1–10.

Alqahtany, S., Clarke, N., Furnell, S., & Reich, C. (2015). A forensic acquisition and analysis system for IaaS. *Cluster Computing*, 1–15.

Beebe, N. (2009) Digital forensic research: The good, the bad and the unaddressed. Advances in Digital Forensics, pp. 17–36. (*Springer*, no.).

Beebe, N., & Clark, J. (2005). Dealing with terabyte data sets in digital investigations. *Advances in Digital Forensics*, 3–16.

Garfinkel, S., Farrell, P., Roussev, V., & Dinolt, G. (2009). Bringing science to digital forensics with standardized forensic corpora. *Digital Investigation, 6,* S2–S11.

Ghaleb, T. A. (2015). Techniques and countermeasures of website/wireless traffic analysis and fingerprinting. *Cluster Computing*, 1–12.

Hu, C., Xu, Z., Liu, Y., Mei, L., Chen, L., & Luo, X. (2014). Semantic link network-based model for organizing multimedia big data. *IEEE Transactions on Emerging Topics in Computing, 2* (3), 376–387.

Hu, C., Xu, Z., Liu, Y., & Mei, L. (2015). Video structural description technology for the new generation video surveillance systems. *Frontiers of Computer Science, 9*(6), 980–989.

ISO/IEC 2012, *27037:2012 Guidelines for identification, collection, acquisition and preservation of digital evidence.*

Jones, B., Pleno, S., & Wilkinson, M. (2012). The use of random sampling in investigations involving child abuse material, *Digital Investigation*, 9: S99–S107. Supplement no. 0.

Luo, X., Xu, Z., Yu, J., & Chen, X. (2011). Building association link network for semantic link on web resources. *IEEE Transactions on Automation Science and Engineering, 8*(3), 482–494.

NIJ. (2004). *Forensic examination of digital evidence: A guide for law enforcement*, http://nij.gov/nij/pubs-sum/199408.htm.

Punithavathani, D. S., Sujatha, K., & Jain, J. M. (2015). Surveillance of anomaly and misuse in critical networks to counter insider threats using computational intelligence. *Cluster Computing, 18*(1), 435–451.

Ribaux, O., Baylon, A., Roux, C., Delémont, O., Lock, E., Zingg, C., et al. (2010). Intelligence-led crime scene processing. Part I: Forensic intelligence. *Forensic Science International, 195*(1–3), 10–16.

Shannon, M. (2004). Forensic relative strength scoring: ASCII and entropy scoring. *International Journal of Digital Evidence, 2*(4), 151–169.

Wei, X., Luo, X., Li, Q., Zhang, J., & Xu, Z. (2015). Online comment-based hotel quality automatic assessment using improved fuzzy comprehensive evaluation and fuzzy cognitive map. *IEEE Transactions on Fuzzy Systems, 23*(1), 72–84.

Xu, Z., Liu, Y., Mei, L., Hu, C., & Chen, L. (2014a). Generating temporal semantic context of concepts using web search engines. *Journal of Network and Computer Applications, 43,* 42–55.

Xu, Z., Luo, X., Mei, L., & Hu, C. (2014b). Measuring the semantic discrimination capability of association relations. *Concurrency and Computation: Practice and Experience, 26*(2), 380–395.

Xu, Z., Luo, X., Zhang, S., Wei, X., Mei, L., & Hu, C. (2014c). Mining temporal explicit and implicit semantic relations between entities using web search engines. *Future Generation Computer Systems, 37,* 468–477.

Xu, Z., Mei, L., Liu, Y., Hu, C., & Chen, L. (2014d), Semantic enhanced cloud environment for surveillance data management using video structural description. *Computing,* 1–20.

Xu, Z., Liu, Y., Mei, L., Hu, C., & Chen, L. (2015). Semantic based representing and organizing surveillance big data using video structural description technology. *Journal of Systems and Software, 102,* 217–225.

Xuan, J., Luo, X., Zhang, G., Lu, J., & Xu, Z. (2015). Uncertainty analysis for the keyword system of web events.

Zhao, L., Chen, L., Ranjan, R., Choo, K. –K. R., & He, J. (2015). Geographical information system parallelization for spatial big data processing: A review. *Cluster Computing,* 1–14.

Chapter 5
Summary of the Framework and DRbSI

The main theme of this research is an examination of the data volume issue affecting digital forensic analysis demands, and to research and propose valid methods to address the increasing volume of devices and data with methodologies encompassed in a framework which is applicable to real world investigation demands. The methods and processes must address the complexity and volume of digital evidence as seen in real world cases. As outlined in the preceding chapters, the proposed framework serves to provide a process flow to enable timely analysis of increasing volumes of digital forensic data. The framework is built upon common digital forensic frameworks, with additional stages of; Data Reduction, Quick Review, and External Source Data input (Fig. 3.1).

The processes and methods were designed using the test data corpus and applied to real world data to ensure applicability with the real world observed number of devices and data volume. The implications of the research relate to providing a method for digital forensic practitioners to process increasing numbers of devices with increasing volumes of data, and an ability to collect and process relevant evidence and intelligence in a timely manner.

The processes are designed to work in conjunction with full forensic analysis, and do not prevent the possibility to undertake full forensic imaging and analysis, which in fact is encouraged should the data reduction and quick analysis process not locate evidence or intelligence, and the framework (Fig. 3.1) and DRbSI methodology (Fig. 4.1) allow for this type of contingency.

The Digital Forensic Data Reduction Framework (Fig. 3.1) outlines and details a methodology for the process of digital forensic analysis, from preparation to conclusion, and provides practitioners with decision points to undertake a rapid review or full analysis, and also allows for the ability to traverse between both methods, or even undertake both methods should the need arise. As has been outlined, if the reduction and review process does not locate evidence or intelligence of value, the framework provides a capability to traverse to full forensic imaging and analysis in a timely manner, which is not seen in other digital forensic frameworks for analysis, such as those of ACPO (2006); McKemmish (1999); NIJ (2004, 2008) which focus

© The Author(s) 2018
D. Quick and K.-K. R. Choo, *Big Digital Forensic Data*, SpringerBriefs on Cyber
Security Systems and Networks, https://doi.org/10.1007/978-981-10-7763-0_5

on evidential analysis of full forensic images rather than including a process of rapid review where appropriate. An advantage of this inclusion is that practitioners can control the speed of an investigation, and if evidence or intelligence is rapidly located, they can move on to the next investigation in a timely manner, which benefits practitioners in an organisation, investigators, victims and suspects (with a timely result), legal and Court staff, and society in general.

Digital Forensic Data Reduction by Selective Imaging (DRbSI) (Fig. 4.1) was developed using research involving test data and real-world digital forensic data holdings, and is applicable to real-world investigations. A method to reduce the volume of data has previously been raised as an issue impeding the application of data mining techniques to digital forensic data, with the conclusion that a method of data reduction was needed to progress rapid analysis (Beebe and Clark 2005; Palmer 2001). The DRbSI process has demonstrated a capability to successfully reduce the original source media to 0.206% of the volume, and still retain key evidence and intelligence information, providing a capability to apply data mining techniques to digital forensic data.

5.1 Conclusion

The number of devices and the volume of data associated with digital forensic analysis have increased dramatically over recent years. This has led to increasing backlogs of work in many digital forensic labs across the globe, and has been described as the "greatest single challenge".

Published literature has approached this topic, with a variety of proposed solutions, yet none that have been able to be successfully applied to reduce the awaiting volume of work, which is ever increasing due to the progress of technology, and the positive response from consumers to embrace new devices. The conclusion of the literature review is that of the many proposed solutions, data reduction has the potential to impact across the entire process of digital forensic analysis.

A framework to guide the process of data reduction and rapid analysis is necessary to ensure the process is applicable in current investigations, and the proposed Digital Forensic Data Reduction Framework has been tested on research data and real-world data and provides for a method to guide the process of data reduction and timely analysis.

The process of data reduction includes the semi-automated selection of key data and files, with rapid review by an experienced practitioner to select data and files which may hold relevant evidence and/or intelligence. The selected files are preserved in a digital forensic logical container, which provides for current and future analysis needs. The metadata from large size video files is collected in a spreadsheet report, and the contents of the video are reduced to key frames in thumbnail format. Large volumes of picture files are likewise collected by reducing the dimension of the pictures whilst retaining metadata stored within, such as EXIF data in JPEG pictures.

In this research it has been demonstrated there is a method to reduce the volume of digital forensic data to 0.206% of the original source data volume, and still retain key evidence and intelligence data. The reduced data subsets provide for an ability to undertake rapid triage, analysis, storage, and historical review. The process of video-thumbnailing provides for a reduced volume of data, and also assists practitioners when presenting this data to investigators, Legal counsel, Court, Judges, and Juries, by enabling a method to print or present the video data.

As outlined, there is a wide range of processes and methodologies discussed which enable practitioners to approach ever increasing volumes of data with confidence that they can collect and process key data to locate evidence and intelligence in a timely manner. The proposed framework includes the ability to move to full forensic analysis should the requisite evidence or intelligence not be located within a data subset, and therefore this process can be applied to a wide range of cases with the knowledge that it may speed up the process of analysis for those cases where the data is located within minutes as opposed to hours, days, or even weeks.

The research method of using test data reflective of real world data, and then applying the methods and processes to real world data ensured the real world applicability of the proposed processes to current cases. The real world application of this research was further demonstrated when real investigations which had stalled, were enabled to continue after using the processes of Digital Forensic Data Reduction. The use of the proposed framework was also beneficial to guide this research, and also applicable in digital forensic investigations to lead them from commencement to completion. Of note was the ability to greatly reduce the volume of data in digital forensic investigations, and the vast improvements in processing times which enables cases to progress within minutes as opposed to hours, days, or weeks.

The Digital Forensic Data Reduction and Data Mining Framework details a methodology for the entire process of digital forensic analysis and provides decision points for practitioners to branch between full analysis and rapid review, which is not present in other digital forensic frameworks.

Digital Forensic Data Reduction by Selective Imaging (DRbSI) is applicable to real-world investigations and provides a way to reduce the volume of data, as demonstrated, to 0.206% of the source volume, and retain evidence and intelligence.

In Volume 2, the Digital Forensic Quick Analysis methodology is outlined, and guides the process of digital forensic analysis to undertake a rapid review of a subset of data, or full forensic image analysis, and addresses a need for a method of analysis which encompasses a range of tools, and can be applied to a range of investigations.

Also examined in Volume 2, is the fusion of digital forensic DRbSI data subsets with external source data to provide a capability to expand the knowledge and value of digital forensic information and data holdings. The DFINT+OSINT process has potential to contribute to a knowledge base of digital forensic data with the opportunity to locate disparate cross-case linkages. When undertaken in a timely manner, this can assist with appropriate resourcing of investigations, with a potential for a timely resolution of investigations.

References

ACPO. (2006). Good practice guidelines for computer based evidence v4.0, Association of Chief Police Officers. Retrieved March 5, 2014, from www.7safe.com/electronic_evidence.
Beebe, N., & Clark, J. (2005). Dealing with terabyte data sets in digital investigations. In *Advances in Digital Forensics* (pp. 3–16).
McKemmish, R. (1999). *What is forensic computing?*
NIJ. (2004). *Forensic examination of digital evidence: A guide for law enforcement*. http://nij.gov/nij/pubs-sum/199408.htm.
NIJ. (2008). *Electronic crime scene investigation: A guide for first responders* (2nd ed.). http://www.nij.gov/pubs-sum/219941.htm.
Palmer, G. (2001). A road map for digital forensic research. In *Report From the First Digital Forensic Research Workshop (DFRWS)*, 7–8 Aug 2001.

Printed in the United States
By Bookmasters